D0506636

KITCHEN
KOMFORTS

KITCHEN KOMFORTS

Fabulous comfort food recipes
and inspiring short stories to nourish
the body and soul

Lulu Roman

CUMBERLAND HOUSE
Nashville, Tennessee

Copyright © 2003 by Three Hearts Snacks, Inc.

Published by
CUMBERLAND HOUSE PUBLISHING
431 Harding Industrial Dr.
Nashville, Tennessee 37211
www.cumberlandhouse.com

All rights reserved. No part of this book may be reproduced or transmitted in any form or by any means, electronic or mechanical, including photo-copying and recording, or by any information storage and retrieval system, without permission in writing from the publisher, except for brief quota-tions in critical reviews and articles.

Cover and book design: JulesRulesDesign
Cover photos: Bob Hailey
Cover art: Marc Giguere
All other photos property of Lulu Roman & Associates

Library of Congress Cataloging-in-Publication has been applied for.

ISBN 1-58182-382-7

Printed in Canada
2 3 4 5 6 7 8 — 08 07 06 05 04 03

Contents

In the cornfield

Foreword

My friends and family have been telling me for years that I should write a cookbook. We have created something rather unique and quite fun for all of my friends and loved ones out there who have supported me all these years. Here is my contribution to the world of food and fun and hopefully "meat for the soul" as well.

I have compiled a collection of stories about my life and cute little things the Lord has given me through the years as well as many fabulous recipes I've had through all of my years as a mom. Some I have just made up myself and some I have gathered from friends and acquaintances. I hope they will feed your soul as well as your family and friends with love and comfort as they have mine.

God has blessed me with such wonderful friends and comforted me with their loyal and steadfast friendship and love. I hope the stories will lift your spirits and bring you a wealth of God's comfort in seeing what He can do in one persons life and realizing He can do so much for you too, if only you will ask Him. He is the bread of life and the living water we all need each day to exist. I pray you will enjoy each page and will return again and again to visit the stories to remind you of how marvelous God's food for the soul really can be.

Lulu, Damon, and Justin

Acknowledgments

To Damon and Justin, I thank you for being the best sons a mom could ever have. Your love has made my life "banana pudding" in times of canned spinach! You are my inspiration to move forward everyday with hope for one more minute with you on this earth. I love you with my whole heart and that's BIG!!!!!

I gratefully acknowledge Marc and Jeanne Giguere for all their loving, caring and dedication to all that is "LuLu Roman's Down Home Parlor Treats", *Kitchen Komforts,* and our "Yummy Food for the Tummy and Soul." You guys rock!

I offer a huge "thanks" to Bob Hailey for his work with all the wonderful pictures, oh you make me look sooo good, Dahlin!

Camille Madeley, you are my angel and my hair always looks like I just flew in from heaven!

To all my friends who gave the recipes you are so fabulous, you are too many to count you know who you are and you are so loved!!!

To Jesus, my provider, my healer, my strength, my friend, my forgiver and my valentine, you are my most valuable treasure and I will live my life in service to you, all my life!

With Archie Campbell on the Doctor set

CASSEROLES, SAUCES, AND SALADS

Jeanne's Tomato Bruschetta with Fresh Basil

2	*large tomatoes, diced*
½	*red onion*
¼	*cup chopped fresh basil, lightly packed*
2	*cloves garlic, minced*
2	*tablespoons olive oil*
1	*large clove garlic, halved*
2	*tablespoons balsamic vinegar*
	Salt and pepper to taste
½	*loaf French or Italian bread or baguette*
2	*tablespoons freshly grated Parmesan*

In a mixing bowl, combine the tomatoes, onion, basil, minced garlic, oil, and vinegar. Season with salt and pepper to taste. Let stand for 15 minutes or cover and refrigerate for up to 4 hours.

Slice the bread in 1-inch thick slices. Place on a baking sheet and rub the cut side of the garlic over the top of the bread, then brush with olive oil. Broil until lightly browned on each side. Spoon tomato mixture over the top. Sprinkle with Parmesan. If the tomato mixture has been refrigerated, broil the bruschetta for 1 minute.

Makes about 16 slices.

Awesome Bow Tie Pasta

1	*16-ounce package bow tie pasta*
2	*green onions, chopped*
1	*6-ounce package Feta cheese, crumbled*
½	*cup balsamic vinegar*
¼	*cup extra virgin olive oil*
2	*cups shopped fresh tomato*

Bring a large pot of lightly salted water to a boil. Add the pasta and cook for 8 to 10 minutes or until al dente; drain and place in ice water to cool. Toss the pasta with the onions, Feta cheese, balsamic vinegar, olive oil, and tomato. Serve immediately or chill 1 to 2 hours in the refrigerator.

Makes 6 to 8 servings.

"I Had A Rough Day" Mac and Cheese

This dish is guaranteed to calm nerves and soothe the soul.

½	*pound macaroni*
¼	*cup butter*
2	*tablespoons and 1½ teaspoons all-purpose flour*
3	*cups milk*
2	*cups shredded sharp cheddar cheese*
½	*cup grated Parmesan*
2	*tablespoons butter*
½	*cup breadcrumbs*
1	*pinch paprika*

In a medium saucepan, cook the macaroni according to the package directions. Drain. In a saucepan, melt the butter or margarine over medium heat. Stir in enough flour to make a roux. Add milk to the roux slowly, stirring constantly. Stir in the cheeses, and cook over low heat until the cheese is melted and the sauce is a little thick.

Put the macaroni in a large casserole dish, and pour the sauce over the macaroni. Stir well. Melt butter or margarine in a skillet over medium heat. Add the breadcrumbs and brown. Spread over the macaroni and cheese to cover. Sprinkle with a little paprika. Bake at 350° for 30 minutes.

Makes 6 servings.

Pot O' Gold Macaroni and Cheese

This dish is so rich and creamy, I save it for special occasions (like Thursdays, Tuesdays, dinner time, etc!!)

1	tablespoon vegetable oil
1	pound elbow macaroni
8	tablespoons (1 stick) plus 1 tablespoon butter
½	cup shredded Muenster cheese
½	cup shredded mild Cheddar cheese
½	cup shredded sharp Cheddar cheese
½	cup shredded Monterey Jack
2	cups half and half
1	cup Velveeta, cut into small cubes
2	large eggs, lightly beaten
¼	teaspoon seasoned salt
⅛	teaspoon freshly ground black pepper

Preheat the oven to 350°. Lightly butter a deep 2½-quart casserole. Bring a large pot of salted water to boil over high heat. Add the oil, then the elbow macaroni, and cook until just tender, about 7 minutes. Do not overcook. Drain well. Return to the cooking pot.

In a small saucepan, melt 8 tablespoons of the butter. Stir into the macaroni.

In large bowl mix the Muenster, mild and sharp Cheddar. and Monterey Jack cheeses. To the macaroni, add the half and half, 1½ cups of the shredded cheese, the cubed Velveeta, and the eggs. Season with salt and pepper. Transfer to the buttered casserole. Sprinkle with the remaining ½ cup of shredded cheese and dot with remaining tablespoon of butter. Bake until it's bubbling around the edges, about 35 minutes.

Makes 8 servings.

Bowtie Pasta with Chicken Demiglaze

Demiglaze:
3   ounces brown gravy
3   ounces beef stock

Pasta:
7   pieces chicken tenderloin
8   pieces artichoke hearts
20   sun dried tomatoes
½   tablespoon garlic, chopped
½   tablespoon shallots, chopped
6   ounces Demiglaze (see directions below)
3   ounces tomato sauce
2   tablespoons peas
2   tablespoon grated cheese (amount hole punched)
¼   cup white wine
1   teaspoon oregano
2   teaspoons basil
½   pound bowtie pasta

Prepare the demiglaze. In a saucepan combine the brown gravy and beef stock. Heat and stir until well blended.

In a large saucepan, sauté the chicken in olive oil. Add the artichokes, tomatoes, garlic, and shallots. Sauté briefly and add demiglaze and tomato sauce. Toss in the peas, grated cheese, wine, oregano, and basil. Toss with the cooked pasta.
Makes 6 servings.

Sweet Potato Casserole

This recipe makes me happy to be a Southern gal!

3   *cups mashed sweet potatoes*
1   *cup sugar*
½   *teaspoon salt*
2   *eggs, beaten*
¼   *cup (½ stick) butter, melted*
½   *teaspoon vanilla extract*

Topping:
½   *cup all-purpose flour*
1   *cup coconut*
3   *tablespoons melted butter*

In a mixing bowl, combine the sweet potatoes, sugar, salt, beaten eggs, butter, and vanilla. Transfer to a baking dish. In a small bowl, combine the flour, coconut, and melted butter and sprinkle over the potatoes. Bake at 350° for 35 minutes.
   Makes 6 to 8 servings.

Misty Rowe, LuLu, Cynthia Gregory, Victoria Hallman, Linda Thompson, Gunilla Hutton, Cathy Baker, and Jackie Waddell

Traditional Wassail
This is a festive drink for the holidays.

1   *gallon apple juice*
3   *cinnamon sticks*
1   *teaspoon nutmeg*
¼   *cup lemon juice*
48   *ounces pineapple juice*
¾   *cup honey*

In a stock pot combine all ingredients and bring to a boil.
Reduce the heat, serve.
Makes about 20 servings.

Fresh Tomato Basil Sauce

8   *pounds tomatoes, seeded and diced*
¼   *cup chopped fresh basil*
1   *large onion, minced*
3   *cloves garlic, minced*
½   *cup olive oil*
     Salt and pepper to taste

In a large saucepan, cook the tomatoes and basil over medi-
um-low heat until the tomatoes are soft. Meanwhile, in a
medium skillet, sauté the onion and garlic in olive oil until
the onions are translucent. Add the onion mixture to the
tomato mixture and add salt and pepper. Simmer on low
heat for 2 hours or until thick.
Makes 8 servings.

Honey Nut Chicken Salad
Can you say... "FABULOUS!"

4   *large chicken breasts*
1   *11-ounce can mandarin oranges or 6 ounces fresh*
     strawberries
1   *bunch romaine lettuce*
2   *green onions, chopped*
1   *cup chopped pecans*
4   *teaspoons honey*

Dressing:
¼   *cup olive oil*
2   *tablespoons balsamic vinegar*
2   *tablespoons white sugar*
½   *teaspoon salt*

Marinate the chicken in either Italian dressing with brown sugar or in teriyaki ginger sauce. Grill until cooked through.

Place the pecans and honey in a nonstick skillet, cook on low heat, and stir until glazed. Don't let the pecans get too brown. Remove and let cool on waxed paper.

Place the lettuce and oranges or strawberries in bowl and arrange the sliced chicken on top.

In a small bowl, combine the olive oil, balsamic vinegar, sugar, and salt. Pour the dressing over the salad and top with the honeyed pecans.

Makes 4 servings.

Hawaiian Pineapple Chicken Salad

This is a very refreshing summer salad. I make it when serving lunch out in my screen porch.

1	*pound cooked boneless chicken, diced*
1	*cup chopped celery*
1	*cup pineapple chunks, drained*
1	*cup mayonnaise*
2	*cups halved seedless red grapes*
1	*small green onion, finely chopped*
1	*cup lemon juice*
1	*teaspoon chopped fresh parsley*
½	*teaspoon celery salt*
	Dash pepper
	Lettuce

In a salad bowl mix all ingredients together. Chill for 2 hours.

Serve on a bed of lettuce, cucumber slices, on a croissant, or on your favorite bread.

Makes 4 to 6 servings.

Buck Owens and my son Damon

Believing in Me

I was filming *Hee Haw* in Nashville in the 1980s when I first went to The Benson Company to meet some of the people in the gospel music industry. There I was introduced to Norman Holland. Norman is almost seven feet tall, with beautiful brown eyes that reflect the compassion in his heart. He was so gentle and kind to me, but I never dreamed we would become lifelong friends.

I invited him to the *Hee Haw* set, and he came to watch us film that week. Norman is quite a funny man with a remarkable sense of humor, and I just love being around him. He has a way of making you laugh when you want to cry, and that is a special gift.

At that time I was signed to Word Records on the Cannon label and had won the coveted 1985 Dove Award for "Best Gospel Album by a Secular Artist." The album was *You Were Loving Me,* which includes "King of Who I Am," a duet with Russ Taff. The song went to number one on the charts and stayed there for almost ten months. Folks still ask me to sing that song today after eighteen years.

Norman and I have become very close friends through the years, and it was he who signed me to the Benson label in 1991. Norman is one of the most accomplished people in the gospel music industry and is therefore sought after by many of the labels. He has been one of the best A&R people for some fifteen years now. Norman is responsible for signing artists to the label and taking care of them, which he is the very best at!

Over the years, Norman has continued to believe in the talents God gave me, and he wants to keep my music in the public eye. I am not the usual gospel singer, as my music is varied and some-times hard to put into a specific category; and, in this industry, as in many, you are sometimes judged by appearance. Norman does not function with worldly attitudes and wants to see the ministry of godly people available to all. He has been a true friend to me in good times as well as tough times. We have laughed and cried together, traveled many miles, and have talked to each other every week, if not every day.

I am honored to say he is one of the closest friends I have ever had in my life, and I will always want to know this gentle giant. He is truly a giant in character, truth, and compassion. He is the one person who has loved and believed in me when I couldn't believe in myself. His steadfast love continues to give me hope and makes me realize the loveliness of God's heart.

Today, Norman is the A&R director for Daywind Records, and I am proud to say he still believes in me after all these years. In God's kingdom, there are those whom He allows to move us to places where we can share His love and message of truth and mercy. I believe Norman Holland is God's gift to my life, as he is the one person who has stuck with me through it all.

I love you, Norman Holland.

Me with my dear friend Norman at Disney World

Appointed Obedience

As a child growing up in a home for orphans, my life and the lives of all the other children were greatly affected by the people responsible for teaching us the things we would carry with us throughout our lives. There was a strict religious atmosphere. We were to attend worship services every time the doors were opened. We had no choice; we were simply told we would go, and that was that. At first, I didn't want to go and, like most children, I would rather have stayed in bed. We all discovered very quickly that sleep was a precious commodity.

I soon learned that the attention I so desperately craved could be found in Sunday school and church. On many occasions, we were given recognition if we made a commitment never to smoke or drink while standing in front of the whole congregation. (No one ever said anything about drugs!)

I was always in that line of children who jumped at the chance to be recognized—for anything! I desperately wanted to be accepted and appreciated, so I was in line every time there was an opportunity to be accepted or approved of. I remember vividly the things that were said from that pulpit. I will never forget how we were informed what was acceptable behavior and what was not. Much of what we were taught came from the preacher. His name was Brother Etheredge, and he was very demonstrative in his presentation of the "gospel of behaviors."

I must interject here that I believe with my whole heart the things I will say now were imprinted into his mind by a prejudiced society devoid of the true nature and love of God. We were told, "Don't paint your face, don't dance, and don't talk to Catholics or

The Orphans' Home where I was raised

blacks." I still hear his voice in my mind as I write today.

Somewhere deep in my heart, because I was always the "fat kid," I felt it was terribly wrong to talk that way about others who were different in some way. I have known the pain of being the "unacceptable one" every day of my life, and although I didn't know exactly what it was I was relating to, I knew the pain associated with being different.

That experience set a pattern in my life to forevermore be kind to those who are different or are told they are "less than" because they don't look the way society says you must look to be accepted.

I detest "societal stupidity." It makes us cater to hate and gives the enemy the power to destroy precious life with Satan's number one tool, deception!

Several years after my salvation experience, I was invited to be part of a large concert in a football stadium in Commerce, Texas. My friend DiAnne and I went to the evening outdoor concert, attended by about five thousand people. It was a chilly evening, and people moved out fast as the concert ended.

As usual, we were sitting at the record table as the people left. We both looked up at the same time and were horrified at what we saw. Coming directly toward us was a very familiar face. We tried to appear as if nothing were out of the ordinary, but I'm sure our eyes must have looked as if they would pop right out of their sockets at any moment as we sat frozen to our chairs. It was James Etheredge, the pastor at the orphans' home. He came directly to me. DiAnne held on to my arm so I wouldn't fall down or run.

He said, "Louise, I don't know if you remember me or not." I said, "Brother Etheredge, I know who you are." Then his weary eyes began to tear up as he told DiAnne and me something remarkable. He told us how for many years he had grieved over the things he had said from that pulpit. He knew he could never get to all the thousands of children he had spoken to during those years, but the Lord had directed him to come and tell me the what he wanted to say to all of us. He repented and asked us to forgive him. He told us he had accepted the Holy Spirit into his life and it had totally changed him.

We forgave him with many tears and hugs and promised to tell everyone we could of his precious act of "appointed obedience."

Cows

I love cows. I don't know exactly why. I just love them—brown ones, white ones, black ones, brown-and-white ones, and especially black-and-white ones. They make me laugh. They make me think of how God must look at us sometimes and laugh. They are bigger than life and hold great value as they give us the milk we need to give strength to our bones and keep us healthy.

Me and my cows

Have you ever just looked into the eyes of a cow? They're really big. And have you ever talked to a cow? Not much response! They're kind of silly-looking with those big eyes, that funny tail, and sometimes those big black spots. It's the spots I love. They remind me of spots in my life I just couldn't remove. Spots of fear, spots of doubt, spots of just not knowing which way to turn on the road of life. Spots I've put myself in when I was too silly to trust God in something small.

He must chuckle at the choices I've made in the small spots of life when I thought I could fix things by myself. Then He lovingly "spots" my debts and my doubts and clears a new place of love and acceptance for me in the pastures of my life. I just love Him, even more than I love cows.

A Healing of the Heart

I was entering a painful transition in my life. I was at the end of a marriage I had hoped would be a lifelong story. I will not put blame on my husband, as I was terribly emotionally ill and needed to be healed of many childhood hurts. We each truly needed healing as he, too, had been extremely abused as a child. We both were experts at "The Hiding Game." I so often hid in my own darkness and distrust that I alienated him from the very deepest places I longed for him to occupy.

One day, as I was trying to make sense of how I would continue my life alone, the phone rang. The caller was the only blood relative I have in my life today. Her name is Cathy Besson, and she is my third cousin. It was around the holiday season, and she and her husband, Clyde, wanted to visit when they came through Dallas on their way to east Texas for Christmas.

I was a bit apprehensive, not knowing her too well, but I was glad to have any relative in my life, in any capacity. She and Clyde had once attended one of my concerts in Houston, Texas, and introduced themselves. They were members of the family that had not wanted me all those years. I vaguely remembered meeting Cathy at her sister's wedding years before, but I had all but blocked that experience from my mind. As was standard practice when my grandmother took me to any event, I was seated in a corner with a TV tray, and people just walked past me and whispered and shook their heads. Now some of those same people were being so sweet and warm and classy. I was really taken by surprise.

We had kept in touch only by mail and phone, so I was glad that someone in my biological family really wanted to know me and my family. I was truly happy to meet Cathy and Clyde, and I will never forget the evening they came to my home. A little intimidated at first, I was soon overcome with joy that would change my life forever.

Cathy was loving and tender. At one point during the evening, she got down on her knees and wept and asked me to forgive her and her family for all the years they had rejected me. It was like a "wash of love" over my wounded spirit. It was the only time in all my life that anyone from the family I had been born into had said they were sorry for pushing me out of their world.

All the years of pain and rejection were soothed by one precious woman's love, which I believe was the one thing that gave me the courage to start the "walk to wellness" I now strive to complete.

This was God's lovely way of giving me permission to move past the pain that had stunted my emotional growth for years.

Today, Cathy and Clyde are pastors and counselors in Jekyll Island, Georgia. We are connected at the heart, and I am so proud to tell everyone I know members of my family. Each day brings anew the joys of acceptance and approval, and my heart continues to bask in the loving respect of one special person who had the courage to ask for forgiveness.

Acceptance with Joy

During the tough times of my life, I often find myself returning to a little book I discovered several years ago. *Hinds' Feet on High Places* is an allegory by Hannah Hurnard. The main character is "Much-Afraid," an orphan. She is being raised by her aunt "Mrs. Dismal Forebodings" and belongs to the "Fearing" family, who are scattered all over the "Valley of Humiliation."

Much-Afraid is very unsightly. Her face is not pretty, her mouth is crooked, and she is also crippled with twisted feet that make her stumble continuously. She works for the Chief Shepherd. Her greatest desire is to go with the Shepherd to the top of the mountains where, in the "Kingdom of Love," she would become perfect and receive a new name and a "whole" body. There she could spring like gazelles with hinds' feet on high places.

The story takes Much-Afraid through countless detours and hardships on her journey toward the fullness the Shepherd will give her, if only she will trust in Him with her whole heart. She constantly must lay down her will and trust in the unknown, making sacrifices all along the way.

It is the most profound book I've ever read. At one point Much-Afraid is in the desert, walking near the desert dwellers' tents, when she comes upon a tiny little yellow flower. It is startling to her, since everything else is dead and brown. She notices an old pipe connected to a water tank from which occasionally drips one drop of water onto the tiny flower. She asks the little flower what her name is, and the little flower turns her face toward the sun and says, "My name is 'Acceptance-with-Joy.'" In that desert, she is the only living thing.

It moved me to tears then and still does. I was at a terribly difficult time in my life. I'd had to admit my grandmother to a nursing home. She hated it and hated me, my marriage was in trouble, and

I was on the brink of another bout with suicide. While visiting the nursing home, my husband met a little lady named "Bunny" whose mind had long been lost. She loved to walk the halls with no clothes on and told my husband she wanted to have his baby.

At one point, she sent a doll home for me to nurse for her. It was so sad. One day my husband came home and threw something on the dining room table, explaining that Bunny had sent me a present. I walked over and picked up a little brown pouch with a snap closure. I opened it, and there in that little pouch was a macramé bead, and glued inside the bead was a tiny yellow flower. It sent me to my knees.

It was such a revelation in my life, a call to remembrance of that unfortunate little flower in the dry desert, whose only hope was for an occasional drop of water. Yet Acceptance-with-Joy was alive and hopeful even in that terrible situation.

It has been ten years or so, and that little yellow flower remains on my dresser. I still have an occasional bad day, but one look at that tiny yellow flower takes me back to the revelation of that day in my life. It reminds me of the journey I someday hope to complete, to the promised perfection of my Savior's kingdom. It is my heart's desire to be "Acceptance-with-Joy," steadfast in achieving my goal: to hear the Great Shepherd say, "Well done, My good and faithful servant."

"For I Know the Plans I Have for You"

There are few days in my life I remember as vividly as September 10, 1950. Although it is not a special date of remembrance on special calendar, it will forever be imprinted in my mind. I was four years old, and my life would be changed from that day forward.

I was wearing a turquoise corduroy jumper with a white shirt and black patent leather shoes. My great-grandmother had very carefully and quietly dressed me that morning and silently put me to the car. We drove for what seemed like hours, to a very large place with many tall buildings where there were children everywhere I could see.

In my three-year-old thoughts, I was happy to see so many children. I hadn't had many friends while living with my granny. She was very strict and lived by one rule: "Cleanliness is next to godliness." I remember that phrase well. She was kind and loved to bake cookies for me; however, she had no patience for dirt. But dirt was my friend! I loved to play in the dirt and make mud pies and throw mud balls at Scrapper, the Dalmatian she kept in the backyard.

When I would get really dirty, she would get really upset. I remember her striving to keep me clean and well-fed, but I have no recollection of anyone holding me or touching me except to change my clothes or wash me. On this day, the silence was deafening.

We drove through a large gate and around to the right of the campus to a two-story red brick building. She parked on the street and took my hand and led me up the massive steps to the huge doors. I remember everything was white as we entered the building. The walls, the uniforms the ladies wore, the beds, the people, and the furniture were all white. I thought it was a hospital. I later learned it was called the "Welcome Home." I heard my grandma tell someone what my name was; then she disappeared into a room. I sat on a white bench and waited for what seemed like forever.

Finally, a lady dressed in white came and took my hand and led me into another room where there were eight white beds along the walls. I was told to change into the pajamas handed to me. I wanted to tell someone that I was going home with my granny. I was curtly informed that my grandma had already left. They tried to tell me she had said goodbye, but she hadn't. I had been dropped off at an orphans' home—abandoned!

For the next fourteen and a half years, I would spend every day wondering what I had done to make my family throw me away. My heart was crushed with devastating thoughts that haunted me for the rest of my childhood. I battled thoughts of being unlovable, unaccepted, and unwanted for many, many years.

I was born with a thyroid problem and for years was the biggest child at the home until another girl came in high school. Because of my size, I was never chosen to play on anyone's team. I was the one who sat and watched all the other kids play and laugh and run. It wasn't until sometime later in my teen years that I had a best friend. I don't think I was really that big then, just big enough to be fatter than the rest of the kids.

I have blocked out the events of many of those years because the memories grew in size (as did I) to become prodigious hurt in my already wounded soul. Harsh words can send a wounded heart hurling down the road to death. I traveled that road for many years, even after I had graduated and left the orphans' home. I now know that the day my great-grandmother left me at the home was a part of God's plan for my life. I know, too, that God equips us with the tools necessary for His will to be accomplished in our lives.

It has taken all my life to realize that the deep hurts and hard places in my life were ordained. I believe that through my broken-ness there had to be birthed a vision. My search for healing has birthed a new identity in me, a place of wholeness and acceptance. Although I am still not perfect to look at, in my healing I hold 20/20 vision of what God allowed so I could live out His plan for my life. I am victorious in His love, love extended to an unlikely, unaccepted child.

The Lord says, "I know the thoughts that I think toward you, thoughts of peace and not of evil, to give you a future and a hope. . . . And you will seek Me and find Me, when you search for Me with all your heart" (Jer. 29:11–13). I still seek His face today, and I grow in His acceptance and approval as I continue to watch Him strip away the bondage that no longer defines me. He has taken the shattered pieces of a wounded heart and pieced them back together with the precious blood of the Lamb to make a lovely pic-ture of mercy and grace with fewer and fewer broken places. I am restored in Him.

This is me at about the age I was
when I was left at the orphanage

BREADS
AND
SPECIALTIES

Cranberry Raisin Nut Bread

1½	cups all-purpose flour
¾	cup packed brown sugar
1½	teaspoons baking powder
½	teaspoon baking soda
½	teaspoon ground cinnamon
1	cup coarsely chopped fresh or frozen cranberries
½	cup golden raisins
½	cup chopped pecans
1	tablespoon grated orange peel
2	eggs
¾	cup milk
3	tablespoons unsalted butter
1	teaspoon vanilla extract

Preheat the oven to 350°. In a large bowl, sift together the flour, brown sugar, baking powder, baking soda, and cinnamon. Stir in the berries, raisins, pecans, and orange peel.

In another bowl, mix together the eggs, milk, butter, and vanilla until combined. Add to the flour mixture, stir until moistened, and spoon into a buttered 9-inch loaf pan. Bake for 55 to 60 minutes or until a tester comes out clean when inserted into the center. Cool in the pan for 15 minutes. Remove from the pan and cool completely on a wire rack.

Makes 1 loaf.

Cheesy Breadsticks

1	11-ounce can refrigerated breadsticks
2	tablespoons mayonnaise
1	teaspoon dried Italian seasoning
¼	cup shredded Parmesan cheese

Flatten the breadstick dough into a 12x7-inch rectangle and cut in half crosswise. Brush with mayonnaise and sprinkle with seasoning and cheese. Separate into strips and twist, using 2 strips at a time. Bake at 350° for 10 to 12 minutes.
Makes 8 breadsticks.

Butternut Squash and Apple Soup

1	2-pound butternut squash, peeled, seeded, and diced
2	Granny Smith apples, peeled and chopped
1	medium onion, chopped
2½	cups chicken broth
1	cup apple juice
½	teaspoon ground cinnamon
2	tablespoons light brown sugar
1	tablespoon lemon juice
1	cup milk
	Garnish: fresh parsley sprigs

In a large Dutch oven or casserole dish bring the squash, apples, onion, chicken broth, apple juice, and cinnamon to a boil. Reduce the heat and simmer for 20 minutes or until the butternut squash is tender. Pour the squash mixture through a wire-mesh strainer into a bowl, reserving the liquid. Combine half of the solids and 1 cup of the reserved liquid in a blender. Process until smooth, stopping once to scrape down the sides. Return the mixture to the Dutch oven.

Repeat the procedure with the remaining solids and 1 cup of reserved liquid. Stir in the remaining reserved liquid, brown sugar, and lemon juice. Bring to a boil, reduce the heat, and simmer, stirring occasionally, for 15 minutes. Stir in the milk and heat thoroughly. Serve in squash bowls if desired. Garnish if desired.
Makes 9 cups.

Blueberry Waffles

1¾   *cups water*
3   *eggs, beaten*
3   *cups golden malted flour*
6   *tablespoons butter, melted*
¾   *cup fresh blueberries*

In a mixing bowl, combine the water with the beaten eggs, add the flour, and mix well. Stir in the melted butter and then add blueberries. Ladle onto a hot waffle iron and remove when golden brown.
  Makes 7 to 8 waffles.

For quick waffles use:

2   *cups complete pancake mix*
1   *cup boxed yellow cake mix*
1¾   *cups milk (add milk until smooth)*

Follow above directions for cooking.

The Culhanes

Cinnamon Raisin Waffles

2   *cups water*
2   *eggs, beaten*
3   *cups golden malted flour*
6   *tablespoon butter, melted*
¼   *cup sugar*
1   *tablespoon cinnamon*
1   *cup raisins*
1   *teaspoon vanilla extract*

In a mixing bowl, combine the water with the beaten eggs, add the flour, and mix well. Stir in the melted butter, mix the sugar and cinnamon together and add the raisins and vanilla. Ladle onto a hot waffle iron and remove when golden brown.

Makes about 8 waffles.

Pure Gold Malted Waffle

2   *eggs. beaten*
1¼   *cups water*
2   *cups Golden Malted Flour*
4   *tablespoons butter, melted*

In a mixing bowl, combine the water with the beaten eggs, add the flour, and mix well. Stir in the melted butter and make sure to mix well again. Ladle onto a hot waffle iron and remove when golden brown.

Makes about 6 waffles.

The World's Best Lasagna

This recipe was handed down to me from my Italian
Mamma, Connie, in New Jersey!

Tomato Sauce:
2   16-ounce cans unprepared tomato sauce
2   6-ounce cans tomato paste (add 6 paste cans of water)
2   cloves fresh garlic, diced
       Salt and pepper to taste
1   teaspoon sugar
½   cup Parmesan cheese
1   tablespoon chopped fresh parsley
1   tablespoon chopped fresh basil
3   tablespoons meat drippings
½   cup browned meat mixture

1   pound lasagna noodles

Meat Mixture: (the same mixture for great meatballs)
2   pounds ground beef
2   cloves minced garlic
1   tablespoon dried basil or 6 leaves fresh, minced
¼   cup Parmesan cheese
¾   cup seasoned breadcrumbs
2   eggs
¼   cup warm water
       Salt and pepper to taste
2   tablespoons olive oil

Cheese Mixture:
15   ounces ricotta cheese
2   eggs
½   cup mozzarella cheese
2   tablespoons parsley flakes
¼   cup Parmesan cheese
1   teaspoons salt and pepper

8 ounces (2 cups) grated mozzarella cheese
       Parmesan cheese for topping

In a large saucepan combine the tomato sauce ingredients, and let simmer for 2 hours.

In a large pot of salted water cook the lasagna noodles. Drain and set aside.

In a large bowl, mix all the meat mixture ingredients except the olive oil until they are blended well. Brown in a large skillet with 2 tablespoons of olive oil. Save 3 tablespoons of the drippings for the sauce. Add ½ cup of tomato sauce to the meat mixture. Set aside

In a medium bowl combine the cheese mixture ingredients.

In a large, rectangular baking dish, layer the sauce, pasta, meat, and cheese mixture until all ingredients are in the dish. The top layer should be meat, sauce, ricotta, and 2 cups of grated mozzarella cheese. Sprinkle with Parmesan cheese and cover with foil. Bake at 350° for 35 minutes.

Makes 6 to 8 servings.

Buckner G. A.'s; LuLu second row far right

Sausage and Hash Brown Casserole

I make this when I have overnight guests. It is simple and a real crowd pleaser!

1   *cup grated Cheddar cheese*
1   *cup sour cream*
1   *10½-ounce can cream of chicken soup*
32 *ounces frozen hash browns (shredded or diced)*
½   *onion, diced*
1   *pound loose breakfast sausage, browned and drained*
    Salt and pepper to taste

Topping:
1   *cup corn flakes*
¼   *cup melted butter or margarine*

In a large bowl, mix the cheese, sour cream, soup, hash browns, onion, sausage, salt, and pepper until well blended. Pour into a greased casserole dish.

In another bowl, blend the corn flakes and butter and spread the mixture evenly over the top. Bake for 45 minutes at 350°.

Makes 6 servings.

The Culhanes with George Lindsey

Heavenly Seven Layer Dip

1	*pound ground beef*
1	*1.25-ounce packet taco seasoning*
10	*ounces sour cream*
½	*head lettuce*
1	*large tomato*
1	*5.75-ounce can pitted olives*
½	*onion, diced*
10	*ounces shredded Cheddar cheese*

In a frying pan brown the meat. Add the taco seasoning as directed on the packet. Simmer for 20 minutes.

In a large baking dish or trifle bowl make layers of each ingredient in the order listed beginning with the meat and ending with the Cheddar cheese. Serve with tortilla chips and salsa.

Makes 4 to 6 servings.

The Culhanes

Adopted

I have visited every state in the U.S. and several foreign countries, ministering in song and word. I love people, and I love being blessed with the honor to be a witness for the God of creation. I have told my story thousands of times in thousands of churches, schools, sports arenas, and open fields. Millions have come after the services and loved me through words, tears, and wonderful hugs. I love this aspect of the gift God has given me in being a public figure of grace and testimony.

In December of 1998, I was invited to the pretty little town of Haleyville, Alabama, for a women's conference. My friends David and Ruth Duncan were involved in the festivities. It was a Christmastime event, and scenery on the stage of the little theater transported us to a wonderful winter day. There were trees decorated in the splendor of a royal Christmas; there was a sleigh and lots of lights; the stage was lit up like a dream. The ladies were beautiful in their holiday attire.

The air was filled with love and thankfulness for one another, and for the opportunity to share this time. I was introduced as though I were the Queen of England. The people stood and cheered and screamed out their love and acceptance to me. It made my heart feel full.

While I sang and spoke, the anointing on the house and on me was evident. I watched as many faces filled with joy and the power of hope filled eyes that had been a bit clouded before that day. The love of Jesus was so moving that morning. Acceptance and approval flowed like a fast-moving stream and soaked us all.

When I sang my last song and started to leave, I was stopped in my tracks. Ruth and some of the ladies had a gift for me. I was pleasantly surprised! I love presents, as I didn't get many as a child. They wanted me to open this large gift onstage. To my utter amazement and joy, it was something I had never received in all my life! It was a certificate of adoption! The town of Haleyville, Alabama, had legally adopted me! The mayor was even there. I was so moved I couldn't stop sobbing. I sobbed trying to get down the stairs. I sobbed going down the aisles, and I still sob today when I think of what that little town did for me. They made me their very own child, a big one at that, but still their own child.

I was physically born in Texas, but now my hometown is Haleyville, Alabama, thanks to a few precious women who wanted to give me the best Christmas present ever. Now, I have the distinct honor of being Haleyville, Alabama's "number one adult child."

I love these people and how they ministered to the one who came to minister to them. They even sent cards by the dozens on my birthday and noted the day in their newspaper.

Haleyville, I love you, one and all.

Bones

Bones are things we usually don't pay any attention to—unless, of course, we've managed to break one. I have been fortunate to have had that experience only once in my life. I broke both my ankles.

I stepped off a two-inch curb the wrong way, and all I heard was two loud "pops." As I went down I remember thinking, Now, Lord, I know You don't want me to have two broken ankles. However, after years of learning that God is the author of good things and not bad things, I know it truly wasn't His will or doing. I spent the next three months in a wheelchair and continued to travel.

Bones are funny-looking things, funny-looking and painful, especially after they have been broken. Bones are the things that literally keep us strong in stature. Some bones are harder than others, and yet they will snap in an instant if pressured the wrong way. In that way, they're sort of like people; we can be strong in substance, yet pitifully weak when pressured.

There have been instances in my life when I thought I was spiritually stronger than I'd ever been, only to find myself pressured by Satan's deceit, to the breaking point. I am thankful the marrow of my strength is the strong arm of an almighty God who is the giver of all life and the true promise to eternal health.

Candles

I don't remember exactly when I began to love candles, although as long as I can recall, I've always had them around me. I love the ambiance they create. Somewhere in my past I must have surmised they made me feel comfortable and secure. I love wonderful smells and used to burn incense for years, sometimes as a cover-up for marijuana when I was heavily involved in drugs.

Everyone in my life has grown accustomed to my love for fragrant candles, as I have hundreds around my home. They make any home radiate with warmth and a sense of comfort. I have candles in the bedroom, in the bath, in the kitchen, in the den, and even on my porch. You can always find a number of them in my suitcases when I travel. They are my favorite gifts to give and get. I love to give the gift of "fragrance" that lasts, and I love to know that someone else will enjoy the fabulous atmosphere they produce.

There have been many occasions when I just needed to light all my candles and listen to music and treat myself to a wonderful time of solace. I note in God's Word there were many uses for candles in Bible times. They were used for everything from sacrifice to search to praise. I feel they make our lives softer, especially around the frayed edges of uncertainty and doubt.

Candles seem to bring a healing of sorts, a temporary "stillness" to a fast-moving pace, a breath of sweetness to the sometimes sour endings of life situations. I light candles in honor of God's goodness and His love for me, as my offering of love to Him. Their lovely lights are also a constant reminder of how much I need God's light in my life, the Light of the World, Jesus Christ. I hope there will be candles in heaven; perhaps some, like the Light of the World, will never burn out.

In Touch

We've all heard someone say, "You keep in touch." We say it when we are leaving, talking, or writing to a loved one. Those words hold such hope of "extension"—hope to see a loved one again or to hear from someone across the miles. Perhaps it is the promise of rekindled friendship or a desire to hang on to the moment that causes us to utter these words.

They cause me to reflect on the way God has touched my life in so many ways. His steadfast love keeps me wanting to stay in touch with Him. His touch birthed joy to a degree unknown at my first call to salvation. His touch to my mind, when I have felt as though I were losing it, has given sweet peace. His touch to my wounded soul has repeatedly reclaimed spaces given to the darkness of depression.

I find in His touch a refreshing splash of life, a cool breeze of comfort in blistering moments of self-pity. Like the touch of His hand to blinded eyes, my life is opened to a vision of incredible sights of newness when I allow Him to touch my self-imprisoned, hard heart.

I still struggle with old hiding places when I can't get out of the darkness quickly enough, and I loathe the weakness I fall into when I move away from His touch. I do know that in the Master's hand resides the only touch that will bring wholeness and health to all who are weary and struggle with self-destructiveness, self–hatred, and self pity. The touch calls us all to benevolence. His grace and mercy are all that satisfies the deepest parts of my longing and desires. I strive to become transparent enough that all who pass through my life feel the desire to "Keep in Touch."

Glory Light

They were two little girls, both in an orphans' home and in a terrible situation. They came to know each other out of complicated need: No one adopted fat kids! One was older than the other by several years. She learned a bit earlier to take the hard knocks of life. Her anger hurled her down the wrong path to destruction and isolation. Her neediness covered sensibility with colors of darkness, masked in drug abuse. Her life became a game, a suicide game.

"Today's a good day to die," were the words that awakened her for years. Unaccepted, self-sentenced to her own prison of "unworthiness," she rode the roller coaster of life with reckless abandon. Believing she was a throwaway, someone's mistake, she gave in to self-abuse, to losing consciousness at every opportunity, mostly to cover the pain of being no one's child. She gave her life to death at every intersection, never dreaming or hoping for answers, only believing she had no right to life or love.

The younger one took a similar path to drug abuse and loneliness in the years after her escape from the orphanage. She watched her parents wound each other to the point of eternal separation. Watching her father leave this world, his words brought a slap of

42

With my precious friend, Diane

reality, a call to wisdom. He asked his children to know God. This would send her on a path of recovery and learning to reach out for love unknown.

As she grew in the love of a merciful Savior, her heart began to mend and fill with love for a friend, lost on a rough and rocky road to destruction. Her prayers resulted in God's putting her directly in her older friend's path. The light of God's love would be the one thing that would stop her friend in her lost tracks, just long enough to look at life!

With a tender heart and strong compassion, she walked with her friend on wobbly legs to a new road, a road that led to healing. A highway to wellness, watching broken pieces of a hardened heart pieced back together with the blood of the Lamb. The light of love would cause her friend to look up—up to glory, to hope, to mercy and grace. This light would bring wholeness and cancel the war that raged in the mind and heart of an abandoned child. It would bring truth, purpose, and a desire to tell others of a healing of the heart only God's love can bring.

Diane and I are still connected to each other today after forty-one years, and I am so thankful she loved me enough to find me again after so many years. We have watched God move in a powerful way in both our lives. We have held each other's children, hung on to each other in times of sorrow, watched as God healed our hearts, and, most recently, watched as He healed my precious friend of breast cancer.

With her husband, Don, and her children, David and Daniel (See "Everyday Mercy"), she has added strength to my life in more ways than I could ever count. We are still basking in the lovely light that saved both of us almost thirty years ago, the light that eases the sting of the war that rages around us, that soothes the pain of loneliness and brings life to hopeless hearts. We understand what it is and have given it our own title. We call it "Glory Light."

Heavenly Reunion

My sons have different fathers. I was not married when my older son, Damon, was born. I had decided that no piece of paper could give me the right to have children at that time, so I just decided to have a child when I wanted one. That was a miracle in itself, since I had always proclaimed I would never have children. I didn't want them to suffer as I had. I told the boys when they were young that they had the right to know who their fathers were, and I would never take that right away from them. I wanted them to know they could have a relationship with their fathers even if we were not living with them. I told them I would never talk badly about their fathers or belittle them.

Even in my marriages, I was confined to my own prison because my emotional state was very unstable for so many years. It was only the empowering presence of God in my life that allowed me to be a good parent, and I asked for His help every day in raising my children. I told them what I believed to be the truth according to God's Word. I was not the perfect parent, but I was surely graced with His goodness to teach me how to love these precious gifts in my life.

I especially love little boys, and to think God allowed me to have two of my own still causes me to tear up even today. Damon was reunited with his father, John, when he was a teenager, and they have a good relationship, even though it's long-distance. Justin wanted to know his father for many years but never asked until my divorce in 1991. By then he had not seen his father in twenty years. We searched endlessly for his father, Gary.

We asked friends on the police force to try to trace him and would get only so far and then hit a dead end. We searched the Internet, and I even looked in phone books as I traveled around the country. I desperately wanted to find him because Justin truly had a major emptiness in his heart. He wanted to know who he was and if he looked like his father or did the same things his father did. I watched his heart grow weary with the absence of a father, and it made my heart hurt to see his hopes dwindle through the years.

We had moved around a bit and were rather hard to track, so we didn't know Gary had been looking for us, too. When my precious friend J. D. Sumner passed away in late 1998, I went to his funeral with my friend Norman Holland. We sat with another friend, Brenda McClain, who had a friend with her. She introduced him as Gene Phillips and laughingly told us he was a spy! I didn't pay much attention to that until we went to eat later, and she again introduced him to someone as a spy. All of a sudden, it hit me. She meant he was a private investigator! We were sitting next to each other, and I almost jumped out of my shoes.

Upon my request to help us find Gary, he was gracious and asked if I had pertinent information he would need. I'd kept just that information with me in my electronic organizer, in case this day ever came. When I got home, he'd left a message on the answering machine that he had found Gary. I couldn't breathe, I was so excited! I had to sit down and literally catch my breath. God had used a wonderful Christian man who was a PI to find Justin's father.

When I called Justin later that day, he said hi, and I told him I loved him and asked if he was sitting down. He said he wasn't, but he could. With a little hesitancy, I said, "I've found him." I didn't have to say anything else; he knew what I meant.

We both broke into tears and screamed and laughed and cried and thanked and praised God all at once. I called Gary later. He was on the road and didn't get my message for several days. It was just before Thanksgiving, and he was headed home for the holidays. At about 11:30 in the evening my phone rang, and the voice on the other end of the phone said, "And just how are you?" I knew it was Gary.

We talked for hours. He owns a small trucking company and travels for a living. He has been happily remarried for eleven years to a wonderful lady named Bobbie who travels with him. Bobbie has two daughters, and Justin has sisters, nieces, and nephews. The girls were excited to have an extended family and were anxious to meet Justin.

Gary and Justin had their first meeting in our home in Nashville on Gary's birthday. Their relationship is so precious and growing by leaps and bounds. They love each other with a deep, abiding love and see each other every time Gary comes through Tennessee. He drives a big rig; on each side of it are three crosses, under which are the words "He Is Risen." Gary and Bobbie are wonderful Christians and trust in God to meet their every need.

We've all spent precious, priceless hours together in the last few years, and Gary's and Justin's hearts are being bonded together in the love of our heavenly Father. I am so thankful for the hope of restoring all the years they lost. I believe God allows these healing events into our lives in His perfect time. Justin graduated from the University of Tennessee at Martin on August 1, 1999, and for the first time in his life, his father and mother were both there to support him in his achievements. We are so proud of him. Damon came home from Germany to be with us, and together we celebrated what God had done for Justin and Gary.

The Word says God will restore the years the locusts have eaten (the years of pain and suffering) to us if we will seek Him. I am thankful we have found through our heavenly Father the earthly father for whom a son's heart grieved many years. It's truly a "Heavenly Reunion."

My favorite picture of Justin
as a teen

With Dale Evans

CROCK POT RECIPES

With such a hectic schedule during my years at *Hee Haw,* and more recently with my concert tours, I had to manage quick dinners for my family after long hours of shooting. I became very skilled at using my crock pot to make some fabulous, "comfort food" dishes. Here they are!

Macaroni Pie

8	ounces macaroni, cooked
3	cups grated cheese
1	16-ounce can evaporated milk
1½	cups sweet milk
2	eggs
¼	cup margarine
1	teaspoon sugar
	Salt and pepper to taste

Combine the cooked macaroni and remaining ingredients and pour into a greased crock pot. Cook for 3½ hours on medium heat.

Makes 6 servings.

Roast (French Dip Sandwich)

3	to 4 pounds beef roast
1	package onion soup mix
1	12-ounce can beer

Trim the fat from the roast. Put the roast into the crock pot and sprinkle with the soup mix. Pour the beer on top of the mixture. Cook on low for about 8 hours. Cut or pull apart to make sandwiches on hard rolls. The juice makes an excellent dip.

Makes 6 to 8 servings.

Chuckwagon Crock Pot Beans

This also reheats beautifully for convenient leftovers.

1	*pound ground beef, cooked and crumbled*
¾	*pound bacon, cooked and crumbled*
1	*cup chopped onions*
1	*cup ketchup*
¼	*cup packed brown sugar*
½	*teaspoon pepper*
1	*teaspoon hickory smoke flavoring*
1	*16-ounce can pork and beans*
1	*16-ounce can lima beans*
1	*16-ounce can butter beans*
1	*16-ounce can kidney beans*

Put all the ingredients into the crock pot and cook on low for 4 to 8 hours. The longer it cooks, the smokier it tastes.

Makes 10 to 12 servings.

My sons, Damon and Justin

Crock Pot Spaghetti Sauce

1	pound ground beef
4	tablespoons cooking oil
1	small onion, finely chopped
1	29-ounce can tomato purée
1	15½-ounce can tomato sauce
1	6-ounce can tomato paste
1½	cups water
1	teaspoon salt
½	teaspoon pepper
½	teaspoon red pepper
½	teaspoon oregano
2	pounds sausage (Italian links or country style)

Brown the ground beef in 2 tablespoons of hot oil in a frying pan. When almost browned, add the onion and continue browning until the onion is tender. Pour the meat and onion into a 3½-quart crock pot. Add the tomato purée, tomato sauce, tomato paste, water, salt, pepper, and oregano and set on the low setting. Cut the sausage into pieces and brown in the remaining oil. When brown, place the sausages in the sauce. Continue cooking for 12 hours. (If you like sauce sweeter, add ¼ to ½ cup sugar to this.)
   Makes 8 servings.

Autumn Fest Minestrone Soup

1	cup diced ham
1	pound corn or chickpeas
½	cup minced onion
1	clove garlic, minced
½	cup diced carrots
½	cup diced celery
1	10-ounce package frozen chopped spinach

1   *10-ounce can tomatoes*
1   *medium potato, diced*
2   *tablespoons chopped fresh parsley*
1   *quart chicken both*
½   *cup elbow macaroni*
     Grated Parmesan cheese

In a crock pot combine all of the ingredients except the macaroni and Parmesan cheese. Add the chicken broth
   One half hour before serving, add the macaroni.
   Serve the soup generously sprinkled with Parmesan cheese.
   Makes 6 servings.

Streusel Pound Cake

I had a hard time believing this would work until I tried it and it was fabulous!

1   *16-ounce package pound cake mix*
¼   *cup packed brown sugar*
1   *tablespoon all-purpose flour*
¼   *cup finely chopped nuts*
1   *teaspoon cinnamon*

Mix the cake mix according to the package directions. Pour the batter into a well greased and floured 1-pound coffee tin. (I have also used an oblong, empty cookie tin. Any tin that fits snugly in your crock pot will work.) Combine the sugar, flour, nuts, and cinnamon and sprinkle over the cake batter.
   Place the can in the crock pot. Cover the top of the can with 8 layers of paper towels. Cover the pot and cook on high for 3 to 4 hours. The cake will slide out of the coffee can and make round slices!
   Makes 8 servings.

Slow Simmered Beef Burritos

2   *pounds chuck roast*
1   *10-ounce can chopped Ortega peppers*
1   *cup chopped onion*
2   *4-ounce cans tomato sauce*
     Flour tortillas
     Refried beans
     Sour cream
     Grated cheese

The night before, begin cooking the chuck roast in the crock
pot. Cook all night.

In the morning, remove the bones. Add the remaining
ingredients and cook on low heat for the rest of the day. Add
the mixture to flour tortillas. Also add refried beans, sour
cream, and grated cheese with meat. Roll up, wrap in foil
and bake at 350° for 10 minutes.

Makes 6 to 8 servings.

Damon, Justin, and ET

Easy Crock Pot Barbecue

This cooks while I sleep and only takes minutes to finalize!

3   *to 4 pounds pork roast*
1   *large onion*
8   *to 10 whole cloves*
     Your favorite barbecue sauce

Before you go to bed, brown the pork in a skillet with a small amount of oil. Peel and slice 1 large onion. Place half of the onion in the bottom of a crock pot. Put the roast in the crock pot and add ½ to ¾ cups water. Add the rest of the onion and the cloves. Set on low.

In the morning, turn off the crock pot, remove the meat, and let it cool. Discard the onion and juices in the crock pot, and tear the roast into small pieces. Put the meat back into the crock pot and add barbecue sauce until the mixture is juicy. Cook on low 2 to 3 hours or until the flavor is blended and hot.

Serve on buns.

Crock Pot Stroganoff

1½   *pounds stew meat, cubed*
1   *10¾-ounce can cream of mushroom soup*
1   *10¾-ounce can cream of French onion soup*
1   *cup water*
     Cooked egg noodles

In a crock pot combine all of the ingredients except the egg noodles. Cook for 5 to 6 hours on low heat.

Serve over a bed of egg noodles.

Makes 6 servings.

Crock Pot Beef Stew

3   carrots, cut up
3   potatoes, cut up
2   pounds chuck or stew beef, cut into 1½-inch cubes
1   cup water or beef stock
1   tablespoon Worcestershire sauce
1   clove garlic
1   bay leaf
1   tablespoon salt
½   teaspoon pepper
1   teaspoon paprika
3   onions, quartered
1   stalk celery with tops, cut up

In a crock pot combine all of the ingredients in the order listed. Stir just enough to mix in the spices. Cover and cook on
low for 10 to 12 minutes, then cook on high for 5 to 6 hours.
More water or beef stock may be added.
   Makes 6 servings.

Split Pea Soup

1   16-ounce package dried green split peas, rinsed
1   ham bone or 2 meaty ham hocks or 2 cups diced ham
3   carrots, peeled and sliced
1   medium onion, chopped
2   stalks celery with leaves, chopped
1   or 2 cloves of garlic, minced
1   bay leaf
¼   cup fresh parsley, chopped (optional)
1   tablespoon seasoned salt or to taste
½   tablespoon fresh pepper
1½   quarts hot water

In a crock pot layer the ingredients and pour in the water. Do not stir. Cover and cook on high heat for 4 to 5 hours or on low heat for 8 to 10 hours until the peas are very soft and the ham falls off the bone. Remove the bones and bay leaf.

Serve garnished with croutons. This freezes well.

Makes 4 to 6 servings.

Tex Mex Potato Corn Chowder

This is a great comfort food with all of my favorite ingredients. I love the creamy, cheesy texture of this soup!

14   *small potatoes, peeled and diced*
1   *large brown onion, finely diced*
1   *green pepper, finely diced*
1   *tablespoon margarine*
1   *17-ounce can cream style corn*
1   *12-ounce can whole kernel corn—do not drain*
1   *4-ounce can diced green chilies*
2   *tablespoons chicken bouillon powder*
    Seasonings (Lawry's seasoned salt, garlic powder, and
    dash of Worcestershire sauce)
2   *cups shredded Cheddar cheese*
1½   *cups shredded Monterey Jack cheese*

Cover the potatoes with water and boil gently, uncovered, until you can pierce them easily with a fork. Drain. In a skillet, sauté the onion and green pepper and add to the potatoes. Stir in the corns, chilies, bouillon powder, and seasonings. Heat until bubbly.

Place the ingredients in a large (5- to 6-quart) crock pot and cook on high until it bubbles again, and then turn to low and stir in the shredded cheese. Simmer on low for at least 1 hour.

Makes 4 to 6 servings.

Thanksgiving Leftover Soup

1	pound cooked turkey, cut in bite-sized pieces
¼	teaspoon pepper
¼	teaspoon oregano
¼	teaspoon basil
3	teaspoons beef bouillon
3	cups boiling water
1	cup (8 ounces) tomato sauce
1	tablespoon soy sauce
1	cup diced celery
1	cup diced carrots
1	large onion, diced
1	cup diced green pepper (optional)
1	cup fresh mushrooms

In a crock pot combine all the ingredients except the mushrooms. Cover and cook on low for 6 to 8 hours.

Add the mushrooms and turn the heat to high for 10 minutes.

Serve with rolls or garlic bread.

Makes 4 to 6 servings.

South of the Border Stew

1	pound lean ground beef
8	cups chicken stock
4	tablespoons all-purpose flour
1	egg
1	red chili pepper
4	medium carrots, grated
5½	teaspoons Minute rice
½	pound spinach, fresh or frozen chopped
½	teaspoon oregano
¼	pound ham chopped
2½	tablespoons parsley

Mix the beef, ½ cup of stock, flour, and egg and form into small balls. Set aside.

Put the remaining stock, chili pepper, carrots, and rice in the crock pot on high to simmer. When simmering, add the meat balls, cover, and cook for ½ hour. Reduce the heat to low and cook for 3 hours.

Add the other ingredients, cover, and cook for 20 more minutes. May be served with lemon wedges if desired.

Makes 4 to 6 servings.

Burgundy Beef Stew

2	pounds stew beef
1	onion, sliced
2	stalks celery, cut in chunks
3	to 5 potatoes, cut in chunks
1	4-ounce can mushrooms (optional)
2	teaspoons salt
2	tablespoons sugar
2	tablespoons tapioca
1	46-ounce can tomato juice
½	cup red wine

In a crock pot place all of the ingredients in the order given, cover tightly, and cook on medium heat all day.

Makes 6 servings.

How Easy Can It Get Vegetable Soup

3   *pounds boneless chuck roast*
1   *large can tomato juice*
1   *box beef vegetable soup starter*
1   *16- to 20-ounce bag mixed vegetables*

Trim all the fat from the roast, and cut in pieces. Place in the crock pot and cook on low heat overnight. Drain off some of the fat from the cooked meat. Add the tomato juice, soup starter, and vegetables for another 3 to 4 hours. Add water as needed. The longer this soup cooks, the better it tastes. Your meal will be ready when you get off work.
   Makes 8 servings.

Spanish Chicken

3   *to 4 pounds chicken, cut up*
      salt, pepper, paprika, garlic salt to taste
1   *6-ounce can tomato paste*
½   *can beer (I used non-alcoholic brand)*
1   *small jar stuffed olives, liquid*

Season the cut-up chicken with salt, pepper, paprika, and garlic salt and place in a crock pot. In a small bowl, mix the tomato paste and beer together and pour over the chicken. Add the olives. Cover and cook on low for 7 to 9 hours. Serve over rice and noodles.
   Makes 8 servings.

Saturday Night Swiss Steak

1½   to 2 pounds round steak (budget cuts of beef may be used)
    Flour
    salt and pepper to taste
    cooking oil
1   16-ounce can tomatoes, cut up
1   large onion, sliced
1   stalk celery, thinly sliced
1   tablespoon bottled steak sauce

Cut the steak into serving size pieces. Coat with flour, salt, and pepper. In a skillet, brown the meat in oil and drain on paper towels. In a crock pot, combine the meat with the tomatoes, onion, celery, and steak sauce. Cover the pot and cook on low for 6 to 8 hours or until tender.
Makes 4 to 6 servings.

French Onion Beef

2   pounds steak, cut into 2-inch pieces
    All-purpose flour
    Pepper
2   tablespoons cooking oil
1   10½-ounce can golden mushroom soup
1   10½-ounce can French onion soup
1   8-ounce package wide egg noodles, cooked

Coat the steak with flour and pepper. In a skillet, brown the steak in the oil and transfer to a crock pot. Purée the 2 soups together to make the gravy smooth. Add the soups, mixing well. Cook on low heat for 6 to 8 hours or until beef is tender.
    Serve over cooked noodles. I throw a few crushed Funions on the top of mine before serving.
Makes 4 to 6 servings.

Beef Italiano

3-	to 4-pound chuck roast
1	teaspoon oregano
1	teaspoon Italian seasoning
1	teaspoon basil
1	clove garlic
¼	teaspoon cayenne pepper
¼	teaspoon salt
½	teaspoon pepper
½	teaspoon sage
½	teaspoon thyme
½	teaspoon marjoram
1	package dry onion soup mix
½	cup water

In a large crock pot, place all of the ingredients and cook on low heat for 24 hours or on high for 12 hours. Shred the meat and serve on crusty Italian Bread. I like to add a slice of Provolone or mozzarella cheese to the top of mine.
   Makes 8 servings.

Overnight Chili with Beans

1	pound ground beef, drained
1	16-ounce can pinto or kidney beans (do not drain)
1	14½-ounce can stewed tomatoes (do not drain)
1	bell pepper (optional)
1	clove garlic (optional)
1	teaspoon salt
½	teaspoon pepper
	medium onion, chopped
2	tablespoons chili powder
1	teaspoon vinegar (optional)

In a crock pot stir all of the ingredients together. Cook on high for 1 hour, then cook on low about 4 hours or cook on low for 5 to 6 hours or overnight. Do not leave on high overnight.

Makes 6 servings.

Makes It's Own Gravy Meat Loaf

2	pounds hamburger
½	cup chopped green bell pepper
½	cup chopped onions
1	cup milk
1	egg
1	packet brown gravy mix
1½	teaspoon salt
1	cup cracker crumbs
6	to 8 potatoes, cut up

Mix the hamburger, bell pepper, onion, milk, egg, gravy mix, salt, and cracker crumbs, and shape into a loaf. Place the loaf in the crock pot and place the potatoes around the loaf. Cook on low heat for 8 to 10 hours.

Variation: Use an 8-ounce can of tomato sauce instead of milk and gravy.

Variation: Add ½ can of tomato sauce to the meatloaf and put the rest on the loaf.

I mash the potatoes and cover them with the yummy gravy from the crock pot.

Makes 6 servings.

Wednesday Night Spaghetti

1   to 1½ pounds ground beef
10   to 14 ounces tomato sauce
1   package meat sauce mix
      Salt, oregano, Nature's seasons to taste
1   cup chopped onion (optional)
1   cup chopped celery (optional)
½   cup mushrooms (optional)
      Spaghetti
      Parmesan cheese

Heat the crock pot as you brown the beef in a skillet. Drain
well and add to the crock pot. In a skillet, sauté the onions,
celery, and mushrooms and add to the beef. Stir in the tomato sauce. Add the package of meat sauce mix and stir in the
spices. Let it cook on low heat all day.

In a large pot, cook the spaghetti and add it to the crock
pot just before serving. Mix well. Sprinkle with loads of
Parmesan.

Makes 6 to 8 servings.

Pot Roast

1   good sized round steak
2   tablespoons all-purpose flour
1   10½-ounce can cream of mushroom soup
1   14½-ounce can stewed or sliced tomatoes
      Salt and pepper to taste

Cut the steak into 1-inch-wide strips and lay them in the bottom of the crock pot. Sprinkle the flour over the meat and
add the soup and can of tomatoes. Season with salt and pepper to taste. Cook on low heat for 6 to 8 hours or on high for
4 hours.

Makes 6 servings.

Super Bowl Chili

1	pound ground turkey
1	pound turkey sausage
2	14½-ounce cans tomatoes
2	16-ounce cans dried kidney beans
1	teaspoon cumin
2	small onions, chopped
1	green bell pepper, chopped
2	cloves crushed garlic
2	tablespoons chili powder
1	teaspoon pepper
	Salt to taste

In a skillet brown the meat and place it in a large crock pot. Add the tomatoes, kidney beans, cumin, chopped onions, bell pepper, garlic, chili powder, pepper, and salt and cook on low for at least 3 hours. This chili tastes best the second day, so I make mine a day early and turn it on to heat up in time for Kick-off.

Makes 6 servings.

The Hagers, Cathy Baker, Linda Thompson, and Damon

Justin's Favorite Beef Stroganoff

1   *1½- to 3-pound round steak*
½   *teaspoon salt*
½   *teaspoon pepper*
½   *teaspoon celery salt*
1   *10½-ounce can mushroom soup or 1 4-ounce can mush-*
        rooms
1   *cup water or tomato soup*
½   *teaspoon steak sauce*
1   *teaspoon sugar*
1   *small green bell pepper, chopped*
1   *small onion, chopped*

In a skillet, brown the round steak and place it in a crock pot.
Add the remaining ingredients and cook for 4 to 5 hours or
overnight. This is good over mashed potatoes or rice.
    Makes 6 to 8 servings.

Crock Pot Stuffed Peppers

1   *to 2 pounds hamburger*
1   *onion, sliced*
¼   *teaspoon salt*
¼   *teaspoon pepper*
1   *egg*
1   *slice white bread*
6   *to 8 green peppers*
1   *16-ounce can whole tomatoes*

In a large mixing bowl combine the hamburger, onion, salt,
pepper, and egg. Pull the bread apart in small pieces and add
to the hamburger mixture. Clean and remove the seeds and
white membrane from the peppers, and stuff them with the
hamburger mixture. Place the peppers into the crock pot and
pour the tomatoes, undrained, over the meat.

Cook on low heat for 6 to 12 hours or on high for less than 6 hours. Any remaining meat mixture can be shaped into a small loaf and cooked along with the peppers in the crock pot. This makes a very hearty meal with a loaf of crusty bread.

Makes 6 to 8 servings.

Crock Pot Barbecue

I like to bring this to covered dish parties. It is a crowd pleaser and very easy to prepare.

1	*5-pound pork shoulder*
1	*tablespoon salt*
2	*tablespoons sugar*
	Pepper to taste
1¼	*cups vinegar*
½	*cup ketchup*
½	*cup hickory smoked barbecue sauce*
½	*tablespoon crushed red pepper*
½	*teaspoon hot sauce*

Trim the skin and most of the fat from the pork shoulder and put it into a large crock pot. Sprinkle the salt, sugar, and pepper over the shoulder, add the vinegar, and cover the mixture. You can cook the mixture overnight.

In the morning, remove the meat from the pot and remove the bones, then mince the meat. Strain the liquid, retaining 2 cups of the liquid. Add the ketchup, barbecue sauce, crushed pepper, and hot sauce and mix with the minced meat. Return the mixture to the crock pot and cook on low until the juice has cooked down to the desired level of moisture.

Makes 8 servings.

No Ordinary Meat Loaf

Sauce:
1   *16-ounce can Hunt's Special tomato sauce*
1   *16-ounce can Hunt's herb tomato sauce*
1   *tablespoon mustard*
1   *tablespoon Worcestershire sauce*
1   *tablespoon sugar (brown or white)*

Meatloaf:
3   *pounds ground beef*
1   *package French's meatloaf seasoning mix*
1   *egg, slightly beaten*
½   *cup cracker crumbs*
2   *tablespoons Worcestershire sauce*
1   *large onion, chopped*
1   *large bell pepper, chopped*
½   *cup catsup*

Combine the tomato sauces, mustard, Worcestershire sauce, and 1 tablespoon of sugar (brown or white). Mix all ingredients together.

In a large bowl combine the beef, seasoning mix, egg, cracker crumbs, Worcestershire sauce, onion, bell pepper, and catsup. Use the top of the crock pot to shape into loaves (should make 2 large or 3 small loaves). Place on a baking sheet and bake at 350° for 45 minutes. Pour off the excess fat.

Stack the meat loaves in the crock pot. Pour the sauce over it. Set on low and cook for 4 to 6 hours. Celery, onion, and green pepper can be added to the sauce if desired.

Makes 8 servings.

Crock Pot Poor Boys
Yes, I said Poor Boys in the crock pot!

3	to 4 pounds boneless chuck roast
1	teaspoon salt
1	teaspoon pepper
½	tablespoon dry mustard
1	tablespoon Worcestershire sauce
½	tablespoon garlic powder
1	large onion, chopped
¼	cup water

Place all of the ingredients into a large crock pot and cook on low heat overnight. Remove the meat and shred. Return it to the juice and serve on Hoagie rolls.
  Makes 6 to 8 servings.

Crock Pot Sirloin Tips
I add a big salad to this meal along with warm dinner rolls.

1	2-pound package sirloin tips
1	cup ketchup
2	tablespoons Worcestershire sauce
1	clove garlic

Cut up the sirloin tips into bite-size pieces. Place all of the ingredients into crock pot. and cook for 8 hours on low heat or for 4 hours high. Serve over rice or egg noodles.
  Makes 4 servings.

Barbecue Beef Brisket

This recipe gives a few of the well-known barbecue places in the South a run for their money.

3	*to 4 pounds beef brisket*
2	*tablespoons Liquid Smoke*
1	*teaspoon garlic salt*
1	*teaspoon onion salt*
2	*teaspoon celery seed*
2	*teaspoons ground pepper*
2	*teaspoons Worcestershire sauce*
1	*cup barbecue sauce*

Place the brisket on foil. Cover both sides of the brisket with Liquid Smoke, garlic, onion, celery seed, ground pepper, and Worcestershire sauce. Wrap and place in a large crock pot. Cook on low heat for 8 to 10 hours.

Remove the brisket and slice across grain. Return to the pot, cover with the barbecue sauce, and cook for 1 hour.

Makes 6 to 8 servings.

Crock Pot Steak Supreme

This is a variation on pot roast but with a beefier texture.

1	*round steak or 8 pieces cube steak*
2	*teaspoons cooking oil*
4	*medium potatoes*
4	*onions*
1	*pound carrots*
1	*stalk celery*
	Salt and pepper to taste
1	*10½-ounce can cream of mushroom soup*
1	*4-ounce can mushroom pieces*

Trim the fat and bone from the steak and brown in a skillet with a small amount of oil or fat. While the meat is browning, scrub or peel the potatoes, onions, carrots, and celery. Quarter the potatoes and other vegetables, the carrots can be sliced. Place the vegetables in the bottom of a crock pot, they take longer to cook. Add the browned steak, seasoned with salt and pepper. Pour the mushrooms over the steak and top with the soup. Cover and cook slowly. You may want to start on a high setting first.

Allow at least 3 to 4 hours to cook. The steak should be very tender when potatoes and carrots are done. We prefer regular round steak, but cube steak or any lean steak is good.

Makes 4 to 6 servings.

My Favorite Pepper Steak

1½   to 2 pounds round steak
⅓   cup all-purpose flour
1   teaspoon salt
1   teaspoon pepper
1   large onion, diced
2   green peppers, diced
1   14-ounce can stewed tomatoes
1   4-ounce can mushrooms, drained
1   14-ounce can green beans, French style, drained
3   tablespoons soy sauce

Cut steak into ½- x 4-inch strips and coat them with flour, salt, and pepper. Place them in the bottom of a crock pot and sprinkle with the remaining flour. Add the remaining ingredients in any sequence. Do not stir. Cover and cook on low heat for approximately 8 hours or high heat for 4 hours. Stir after just 2 hours.

Serve over rice.

Makes 4 to 6 servings.

Crock Pot Chops

This was always a nice dinner to come home to after a long day of shooting *Hee Haw*.

6   *pork chops*
1   *10¾-ounce can chicken noodle soup or chicken with rice*
1   *4-ounce can mushroom soup*

Brown the pork chops in a skillet. Place the browned chops in the crock pot, and add the mushroom soup and chicken soup. Cook for approximately 6 to 8 hours.

Note: You can double everything if needed. You may substitute the pork chops with country style pork ribs.

Makes 6 servings.

Burgundy Beef Stew

1   *pound stew beef cubes*
½   *cup red wine*
4   *to 6 carrots, cut up*
10   *to 12 pearl onions*
4   *to 6 potatoes, cut into cubes*
2   *cloves garlic*
1   *teaspoon Worcestershire sauce*
2   *tablespoons soy sauce*
     Salt and pepper to taste

Brown the stew beef cubes (you can coat them in flour) in a skillet. After they are browned, put them in a crock pot. Deglaze the pan with ½ cup red wine and pour into the crock pot with the beef cubes. Add the cut-up carrots, onions, garlic, and potatoes along with the Worcestershire sauce and soy sauce, and cook on high heat for 4 hours. Add water as necessary. Season with salt and pepper to taste.

Makes 6 to 8 servings.

Honey Ribs and Rice

These ribs are so tender they fall off the bone.

2   *pounds lean spare ribs*
1   *14½-ounce can condensed beef stock*
½   *cup water*
2   *tablespoons maple syrup*
2   *tablespoons honey*
3   *tablespoons soy sauce*
2   *tablespoons barbeque sauce*
½   *teaspoon dry mustard*
½   *teaspoon ginger*

Bake the ribs at 350° for 1 hour (½ hour per side) or broil for 15 to 20 minutes to remove the fat. Cut them into single servings. Combine the rest of the ingredients in a crock pot and stir to mix. Add the ribs. Cover and cook overnight or on low heat for 8 hours. Remove the empty bones. Serve over rice.
Makes 4 to 6 servings.

Damon

Crock Pot Roast Beef

If I put this in the crock pot on high before Sunday morning church, it is usually done in the afternoon when we get home.

5	*potatoes, peeled and quartered*
3	*carrots, peeled and quartered*
1	*10½-ounce can cream of celery soup*
1	*10½-ounce can cream of mushroom soup*
1	*package dry onion soup mix*
1	*soup can full of water*
1	*medium-size beef roast, browned on both sides*
	Salt and pepper to taste

Place raw vegetables in crock pot. Mix the soups, soup mix, and 1 can of water together and pour over the vegetables. Place the roast on top. Cook on high for 3 to 4 hours. If you use canned vegetables, put the meat on bottom, the vegetables next, and then the soup mixture.

Makes 6 servings.

The haystack

What You Confess

She had long, wavy, natural red hair, beautiful eyes, and a lovely smile. She was the first really close friend I would have after my escape from the orphans' home. She was classy and brash and not afraid of anything. She knew how to dress to get the attention she needed at the moment. Her name was Cheryl. She taught me many things, mostly how to make it in the world I had run to after being caged up all my life. She was wild and reckless, and I loved her because she was the first taste of real freedom I ever knew.

We went to places I'd never dreamed existed. I was truly green when I jumped out into the world from the fenced areas to which I had long been remanded. Cheryl showed me things I've kept with me all my life, things like the art of caring for others. That was something she was an expert at. She had a wonderful way of taking care of others' needs. The only problem was, she couldn't seem to hold on to those she loved for very long.

Being emotionally troubled much of the time, she found herself alone while her three babies were in someone else's care. At that age, I didn't know what the ramifications of that could be. I knew she loved her children. She talked of them constantly, carried pictures around to show everyone, and brought the children to our apartment when she could.

She must have been a wonderful mother before her troubled mind took control, because it was she who taught me how to care for my babies. She taught me how to clean and feed and hold my precious Damon when he was first born. She gave me the baby shower all new moms deserve, even though I was alone. I knew she was troubled; I didn't learn how badly until years later.

We traveled the roads of abuse and recklessness with a vengeance, never stopping to look at where we were headed. We made it to all the "rock festivals." Drugs were on our main menu. We talked of how we wouldn't live to be thirty years old. It was kind of a joke between us. We talked about how life was horrible enough that we didn't want to live past thirty anyway.

When I gave my heart to Jesus, Cheryl was the first one I wanted to go back to and tell of my rescue. When I talked to her, she was sad, totally uninterested, and told me she had plenty of time. I went to Israel a few months later with my church group, and while I walked where my Savior had walked, she lost her life to drugs. They found her hanging over a door and called it suicide. I believe she was murdered.

I was horrified to learn of Cheryl's fate when I returned to the States. Her words will forever ring in my spirit: "I've got plenty of time." I pray in those last few moments of life she reached for the Savior's hand to lead her into eternal, abundant life.

The Word of God clearly says, "What you confess with your mouth shall be yours." As young girls, we both confessed death, and today my heart remains heavy with the grief of losing my friend. We must learn to confess life and health and wholeness. We must take hold of God's promises for our lives and deny the enemy's deception that robs us of precious life.

Declaration

In the early years after my conversion, I had thousands of invitations to visit churches to sing and give my testimony. One of those occasions will forever hold a dear and special place in my heart. I had been invited by Rex and Maude Aimee Humbard to the Cathedral of Tomorrow in Akron, Ohio. I decided to take my long-time friend Diane with me.

It was the largest church I had ever seen, with all the newest technological equipment. Diane and I were giddy with excitement just to meet Rex and Maude Aimee. Having regularly watched their television programs before we met, I already sensed in my spirit that there was something awesome about these people.

The church was breathtakingly beautiful, and all the assistants were more than accommodating. A "sweetness" hung in the air that I had not experienced before. We were taken to the makeup room first, where Maude Aimee was having the finishing touches put on her hair. Diane and I both were so impressed, all we could do was gawk and giggle. Then we were taken to Rex's office to wait for my time to sing and testify.

We watched on the TV monitors as the program started. The spirit in that room was like showers of heavenly balloons bursting with new life over everyone. Then Maude Aimee stood and began to sing "More About Jesus." It was so anointed it made us weep. I was a basket case by the end of that song! I had to mop up before I could go out to sing.

It was the first time I would tell my story on national television. As I sang and testified, the power of God was all over me, and many were touched. Thousands have told me they saw that program on a cold winter day when the snow kept them from going to church, and it changed their lives.

I know it was God's plan for many to see that television program. When the service was over, we went into Rex's office, and in a few minutes he came in. I will never forget what he did. I was sitting in a large chair, and he came over to me, got down on his knees, and began to weep. He thanked me for being willing to share my story of deliverance from drugs and for telling the world that Jesus can give life to dying souls. Then he said, "Sweetheart, today you talked to more people than Jesus ever did in His whole life." It was a staggering declaration that made me burst into tears.

I realized for the first time that day the magnitude of what God was doing with an unlovely, unwanted, unacceptable life. With his words, Rex opened my heart to the reality of what God was doing in my life. I was called to help others who felt unworthy because of the world's harshness toward imperfection.

It has taken me years and years to understand the plan God has for my life and how it will directly affect others. My prayer is that in reading these pages, you will come to know how much God wants to love you. He can help change your self-image to reflect the whole person He created in you, if you will but trust in Him.

Indelible Imprints

I don't know much about the family I was born into. Answers were never available to me. They must have been too painful to reveal. I did know my grandmother, my great-grandmother, and a couple of aunts. I vaguely know my birth mother; she was an unfortunate child of terrible and extreme abuse, and thus was emotionally unable to enter the mother-child relationship. I do not hold that against her, although I would have loved to know the person she might have become had she not been so physically abused to the point of mental unavailability.

When I was allowed to leave the orphans' home one weekend per month and for some holidays, I spent the most time with my great-grandmother, Imogene Roche. She was short in stature and had a great big heart. Not much of a talker, she was a precious doer. I remember how she would bake cookies and cakes and take me to the Texas State Fair and to the Methodist church. I blocked out so much of my childhood that I don't remember much except those few special moments. After she passed away, my grandmother gave me a picture of her. It is one of those rare treasures I have in my possession today; it tells a poignant story.

My great-grandmother is in the bottom right-hand side of the photo, looking up. In one hand is a crumpled telegram; the other hand is touching a globe. To the left is a framed photo of a young man in a military uniform. Beneath his picture lies a stack of war bonds; above the globe is the infamous picture of Iwo Jima. The soldier's name was John W. Smith III. He was one of the young men who died there on that hill, raising that flag. This was her grandson and my cousin. I never knew him, but the picture is remarkable. It leaves an indelible imprint of our brave young soldiers on all who view it.

It is the kind of imprint the cross of Calvary has left on all humankind. The sacrifice of the bravest life in all of history. Love so amazing it reaches far past war and rage, hate and grief, to allow birth in death given as the unmerited favor of a merciful Savior. A remarkable image of grace given in love so amazing, it leaves the indelible picture of unconditional love to every heart who will receive it. Picture perfect!

Destination: Bountiful

It all began when I saw my friend Mark Lowry at a PrimeTime Country taping. We talked about Bill Gaither being on the show and how the Gaither videos had been such a blessing to thousands. I told Mark how I watched with tears the precious moments captured on tape for all God's children to enjoy. I expressed a desire to be part of this very sacred, anointed, beautiful family of servants.

Well, Mark just jumped up and went and got Bill, and they came into my dressing room to invite me to be part of one of their tapings. I wanted to sing the "Hallelujah Chorus" and fall on my face at the same time. I held this promise in my heart with such anticipation, never dreaming what it would become to my life.

In March, I came home to a message from Bill on my answering machine, inviting me to come to Indiana for the next taping, which was scheduled April 7–9. He would call again and talk to me in person in the next few days. I felt so honored and awed to have one of the greatest privileges I could ever hope for. On April 7, Norman Holland (one of God's most precious gifts to my life), Celeste

Winstead from my record company, Daywind, and I set out on our journey. Jerry and Dottie Leonard blessed us with their new Lincoln to drive, and we were off to Alexandria, Indiana.

It was five and a half hours of great fun. We laughed, sang, ate, ate, ate, and laughed some more. Celeste is great fun, as well as being very proficient in her job skills. We arrived at about 3:00 P.M. and checked into the hotel. I was just buzzing with excitement. We had about an hour or so before we were to be at the studio.

Upon arrival, it looked like Disney World. Buses were everywhere, not to mention the cars and people. We went into Mr. Gaither's office and met Connie, his secretary, and some of his staff. The anointing was dripping off all of them. I wanted to do a rain dance or something to express my joy! We were issued our badges (for security purposes) and immediately ushered into a large warehouse where a fabulous hot meal had been prepared for us. What a great beginning. Eating with the saints! Oh, yum!

After we ate, we were seated in the studio. As I looked around the room, I was overwhelmed to be in the middle of such marvelous people. There were Howard and Vestal Goodman, the Cathedrals, J. D. Sumner (whom I sat next to and who kept me in stitches), Joel and LaBreeska Hemphill, The Nelons, The Martins, The Speers, The Blackwoods, Big John Hall, Cynthia Clawson, Janet Paschal, Tonya Goodman-Sykes, Candy Hemphill-Christmas, Jake Hess, Mark Lowry, Geron Davis, Jeanne Johnson, Jessie Dixon, Henry and Hazel Slaughter, and literally hundreds more, each one precious and anointed.

It was like having a preview of heaven's choir when we all began to sing. It took my breath away and made me feel so special. The tears started right then and didn't stop for the next three days. I had the most awesome vision of thousands of angels slamming into one another, trying to find space in that room and wanting to sound like that glorious group of saints. Oh, it was awesome!

Bill introduced each one, each group as if they were his very own. I noticed the look on his face right away. It was as if he were looking at his own children get up to sing for the first time. I've never witnessed that before. The joyous songs of Zion were lifted up to the throne room, and I was getting to participate with these precious singers and writers and ordained ministers. I knew this was the closest I'd ever be to that heavenly sound I feel in my spirit when I worship my Lord.

Every singer and every group of singers was precious. The power of God was thick in that studio. Forgiveness ran rampant.

Hearts were mended from years of hardheartedness and jealousy. Relationships were renewed, loving arms birthed newness of life, watered with hope and mercy. The healing continued for the three days we were bonded together.

There were moments when God"s heart flowed out from precious older vessels who have been faithful servants for some fifty to sixty years. I was drenched with waves of joy and hope for a continued life of "Shining the Light" to all nations. They were pliable even in their weariness, the light still shining brightly through tired servants' eyes. I will forever be moved by the memory of witnessing those precious saints and their love for a merciful, loving God who has walked every mile so close to them.

It is my desire to be like them when I am sixty years into service for my King, ever loving Him, ever trusting, ever holding on to God"s unchanging hand to lead me through. I'd never been to a Gaither taping before, so everything was new to me. Bill invited young people, children who blew us all away, beautiful little girls who sounded like angels, a young man with a real gift to sing and minister at such a tender age. There were wonderful witnesses from many races, and I was touched by the love and acceptance of each of them.

The Galileans were there praising in multiple languages. The Bennett Sisters and Charles Johnson were a blessing in abundance to all. It was a heavenly dessert of many fruits, and we all inhaled every word and note of praise. Jessie made me want to dance more than once. We prayed together, cried together, laughed together, ate together, and were mended together by the healing bond of God's love. I have never had the privilege of going to a family reunion of my own family, as I grew up in an orphans' home, but I now can say I now know what that must be like. It's so exciting, so much fun, so moving and mending. I was so blessed to have many experiences that I will hold in my heart forever.

At one point, I was led to give a brief testimony some had never heard. I spoke of not having a family or memories most people have of childhood times; of not knowing the loving embrace of anyone as a child or even having a bicycle or a doll that I remember. I felt like I was home. After that session, Jake Hess came over to me and put his precious hands on my face and asked if he could be my big brother. It took my breath away. J. D. also said he'd be my brother; so did George Younce. Janet and LaBreeska said they'd be my sisters! So many came to me and spoke precious "welcomes" to the family. Several times Gloria reminded me to never feel alone because I now belonged to their family.

I am still so moved to acceptance, I can hardly speak aloud of these precious moments without sobbing with gratefulness. I am covered up with a loving family, and I will grow with the knowledge that these precious ones are my heritage.

I am bathed in blessings for this incredible experience to my life. I offer praise to a loving Father who extends His life to me through the blood of the Lamb, my Savior, Jesus Christ. I have returned home to a full knowledge that I am far more favored than most to have been given the privilege of being a part of this extraordinary journey to bountifulness.

I honor my mentors Bill and Gloria Gaither, as they have honored me with the experience of a lifetime. I will forever be reminded of God's unconditional love to us all as I replay the videotape of the Homecoming episodes. It has been the joy of my heart to "Sing With The Saints" and be with precious "Old Friends."

Driving

Every parent encounters that fateful day when it's time to teach the firstborn how to drive. This is usually accompanied by much fear and trepidation! I remember well my experience with my firstborn, Damon. First, I got to spend several months "shuddering" in anticipation of the dreaded sixteenth birthday and all the questions that accompany this monumental event. Then I got to decide just which car the "event" would take place in.

I have always loved Lincoln Continentals and have been blessed to drive one most of my adult life. This is not a car in which you want to teach anyone to drive. Therefore, I decided to let Damon have this wonderful experience in someone else's vehicle. We were living in Texas and had a large area of land around us, so I thought that would be a good place to start.

Damon was so hyped up, he was up and ready at seven in the morning. I thought it would be wise to demonstrate some things that would be important for him to know before his first driving experience. He flatly informed me that he knew exactly what to do, so it was just as well that he take the wheel first.

I crept around to the other side and slid into the passenger seat, hanging on to the seat with every ounce of faith I could muster. He jumped in, put that gear in reverse, and squealed out of the driveway with me screaming, "Jesus, help us!" at the top of my lungs.

He just grinned and floored it. He took off like he was Jeff Gordon leading the pack. I was horrified.

All I could do was pray and scream and scream and pray. He flew around city blocks like the west wind, and I just continued to scream. He jolted to quick stops for stop signs, then gave me a cute little look and kept driving. I thought I would have a coronary for sure; he drove like he had been a racecar driver all his life. I just knew I was going to die that day!

Damon's father, John, had allowed him to take the wheel on several occasions, and Damon thought that was all he needed to know, that he could hold the wheel and stomp on the gas pedal, and things would work out. I wanted out of that car, out of that situation, and out of the smoke we left at each turn.

Now when I think about that day, all I can do is laugh and praise God we made it through that harrowing experience. Damon laughs and still has that little gleam in his eye when we remember that day. I think of how we can get so far ahead of God's will in our lives and how He must sometimes laugh at our silly exuberance for things of which we have no knowledge. He loves us so much that He holds our future in His very eyes.

I marvel that His plan for our lives always brings a lesson in patience. We simply have to learn to hang on in the uncertain times and trust in His plan, knowing He has the best in store for us if we will just allow Him to guide us. For He truly is the driving force in all of life.

Everyday Mercy

He looked so small, sitting there in the middle of that big hospital bed. His hands shook just a little, his head upright, legs crossed. He seemed too calm, even though he wasn't exactly sure why he was there.

When his mom came into the room, when his dad talked to him in a whisper, his big blue eyes were always looking up. Doctors and nurses, family, friends (and there were lots of them)—were always met with those clear blue eyes. Eyes filled with hope, searching for mercy, every second, every day.

Although he was surrounded by love, he still looked for mercy, for grace that would cover a frightened child's worry about the next minute, of tomorrow. There was a large mass in his chest; they called it T-cell leukemia. Lots of loved ones rushed to the throne room in prayer, calling out for mercy, healing, and comfort. In twenty-four hours, it was evident the Master's hand had touched him in a mighty way; it was a mercy touch. No mass—not that day. Mercy had won the day.

In the days and months and years that followed, mercy surrounded those beautiful blue eyes, always looking up. Always looking to a loving mom's heart for strength to make one more round of medical tests, to a strong dad for courage to endure yet another prod or poke somewhere in that small body.

Daniel

Looking to a heavenly Father for assurance that He was still there with mercy, with grace . . . every day. Today, my friend's son Daniel is eighteen. He stands six feet tall, free of leukemia; but he still has those beautiful blue eyes, still strong in mercy, the everyday kind.

"Is That All There Is?"

It was Christmas in Texas and another hot one. We were living in the brand-new house I had just bought. Financially, I was doing quite well; the house was very big and expensively furnished. I have always strived to be a giver in my life and wanted to bless my children with everything I never had. The year had been good, and I wanted to shower them with presents.

We got up early Christmas morning and went into the den to open gifts. The tree was absolutely loaded; I believe the boys each got about twenty-five presents. It was with great joy I watched them open package after package. They went after it with a vengeance. Paper flew wildly in all directions. They barely got one opened before they dropped it to move on to another one.

*Justin and Damon with Santa
as young boys*

I loved the idea of giving them everything they wanted. It made me happy to see them happy. After opening the last gift in his pile, Justin declared, "Is that all there is?" It shocked me and made me think right then, What have I done? I looked at him with a smile and said, "Yes, darling, that's all there is." I didn't lay any blame on him; it was all mine.

Throughout the years of my life, I have given anything and everything I could to be accepted, thinking it would make someone love me or want me. This was a great revelation to my life. I later explained it to the boys and told them that even though they'd had an incredible Christmas, what I had done was wrong. It took some time for that piece of information to sink into their minds, but I am proud to say that it did. We can learn through our mistakes if we will allow ourselves.

I learned through that experience, and others, that it is wrong to try to buy love or friendship. It is so important to teach your children that they need the experience of working for what they want because it brings self-worth to their lives and builds character.

I am thankful today that I don't need to barter my soul for acceptance. God's love is the acceptance that is still bringing me to terms with who I am in Him. His love is a resting place for weary souls who question, for in His love there is no questioning. When you receive that revelation, that's all there is!

James Ryle

I have been blessed by being able to stay in touch with several of the friends I grew up with in the orphans' home. Some of the girls and I correspond several times a year via e-mail and snail mail. It is so rewarding to see that some have remained connected through all these thirty-four years.

I was able to attend our thirtieth reunion. It was the first time I had been back to the orphans' home. It was terrifying to go, but it turned out to be a truly precious time that settled some areas of my memory. I had a chance to see nearly all the members of my class of 1964.

Dear friends were anxious to see me, and the feeling was mutual. It was good to once again be with Betty Jean, Emma Lee, Gracie, Cynthia, Gwen, Gladys, Edna, Alan, and Mary Lou, to mention just a few. I have not been able to return for any other reunions, as my schedule has kept me busy with travel on those dates for ministry events. I will, however, have a chance to go to the one-hundredth anniversary of the home in October of 2003.

After moving to Nashville in 1991, I attended Abundant Life Church, where I got a wonderful surprise. James Ryle, a noted pastor and chaplain for the Denver Broncos, was scheduled to speak at our church. I thought, This couldn't be the James Ryle I knew growing up in the orphans' home, but I soon find out that it was. His sister Valerie, who was older than we were, became one of the best friends I had before I graduated. It was so funny to think that this little "rascal" I had known was now a powerful man of God.

Our reunion at the church was a wonderful time of fellowship and memories. James had taken a road to disaster after running away from the home and spent time in prison for his mistakes. He had run from God's call on his life for many years and finally gave in to it. He is one of the most prolific, knowledgeable, and gifted pastors I have ever known.

We both have vivid memories of the harshness of some of the treatment at the orphans' home. I need to explain that most of us came from broken homes, and there were hundreds of children there. Many people worked at the home only because they needed a job, not because they were qualified to work with children. Thus there were incidents of abuse.

When I look back now, I realize most of the people who worked there did the best they could. There were so many children, and time was limited for getting all the chores done, which left little or

Me with James Ryle

no time for individual attention. The living conditions were hard. There were sometimes six to eight children in one room, with no privacy and no choice of whom you spent your life with. Discipline was harsh—sometimes too harsh.

Diane was beaten nearly to death by one of the house-mothers, who was fired over the incident. Memories were not the best for a child left alone and scared. There were those who were kind and caring and did the best they could with so many mouths to feed and chores to supervise. They did try to present a Christian environment, although it was strict, with no room for error.

On one occasion, as James and I stood in the front of the church talking, a young lady came up to us and began to tell a story that would affect both of us. Jan Fletcher was a member of our church. She began to cry and told us that she was the great-granddaughter of the man who had started the orphans' home in the early 1900s. His name was Robert Buckner. She was sincere and wanted us to know how badly she felt about what we had gone through in the home. She asked us to forgive her whole family for the injustices we had suffered. We both were taken by surprise and immediately told her how nice she was to come and inform us of her family connections.

Forgiveness is sweet healing and always welcome in the family of God. It was a night of healing for both James and me, and for Jan as well. James and I look back now on those times and hold no bitterness or resentment. We are certain of God's plan for our lives.

We know that the two of us survived our childhood because we were ordained to be the servants God called us to be. James Ryle is a precious friend and still influences thousands today with his knowledge and counsel. He pastored the Boulder Valley Vineyard, in Boulder, Colorado, for more than twenty years and now lives in Nashville and leads Truth Works Ministries. He is a teacher extraordinaire and travels the world.

MEATS
AND
MAIN COURSES

Here are some yummy and different things you can make for dinner. I love them all! You'll notice a lot of chicken recipes because I just love chicken, but you can substitute beef or pork for any of these dishes and they'll still leave you smacking your lips with delight!

Pork Tenderloins With Cranberry Relish

1	*large oven bag*
2	*tablespoons all-purpose flour*
1	*8-ounce can jellied cranberry sauce or 1 cup whole berry sauce*
½	*cup sweetened dried cranberries or raisins*
⅓	*cup firmly packed light brown sugar*
2	*tablespoons white vinegar*
1	*teaspoon ground ginger*
1	*to 1¾-pounds pork tenderloins*

Preheat the oven to 350°. Place an oven bag in a 13x9-inch baking dish. Add the flour to the oven bag, twist the end of the bag, and shake to coat. Add the cranberry sauce, cranberries or raisins, brown sugar, vinegar, and ginger to the oven bag, squeeze the bag to blend the ingredients. Add the pork tenderloins, turning to coat. Arrange the ingredients into an even layer, close the oven bag with the nylon tie, and cut 6 ½-inch slits in the top of the bag. Bake for 40 to 45 minutes.
   Makes 6 servings.

Home-Style Vegetables

1   small oven bag
2   tablespoons all-purpose flour
4   small red potatoes, cut into fourths
1   16-ounce package frozen cut green beans
2   carrots, cut into eighths
1   10½-ounce can condensed chicken broth
2   garlic cloves, pressed
1   teaspoon dried basil
    Fresh basil sprigs for garnish

Preheat the oven to 350°. Place the oven bag in a 13x9-inch baking dish. Add flour to the oven bag, twist the end of the bag and shake. Place the potatoes, green beans, carrots, chicken broth, cloves, and basil into the bag and shake well. Close the bag and lay it in the baking dish. Bake for 40 to 50 minutes. Garnish with fresh basil sprigs

Makes 4 to 6 servings.

The Truckstop set with Gaylord Sartain and George Lindsey

Thai Chicken Sate with Spicy Peanut Sauce

4   *boneless, skinless chicken breast halves*
2   *tablespoons orange juice*
2   *tablespoons soy sauce*
¼   *teaspoon sesame oil*
1   *large clove garlic, minced*

Spicy Peanut Sauce:
2   *tablespoons finely chopped fresh cilantro*
3   *tablespoons warm water*
3   *tablespoons peanut butter*
1   *teaspoon brown sugar*
½   *teaspoon crushed red pepper flakes*
½   *teaspoon soy sauce*

Cut each breast half into 8 cubes. Thread 4 cubes of the meat onto each of 8 skewers and place them in an ungreased shallow dish or a 13x9-inch baking dish. In a mixing bowl, combine the orange juice, soy sauce, oil, and garlic and mix well. Pour the mixture over the chicken, let it stand at room temperature for 15 minutes, turning once.

In a small mixing bowl, combine the sauce ingredients and set aside. Line a broiler pan with foil and broil until the chicken is no longer pink, turning once. Serve immediately with sauce.

Makes 4 servings.

Skillet Apricot Chicken

2	tablespoons all-purpose flour
½	teaspoon salt
¾	teaspoon garlic
¼	teaspoon ginger
3	pounds chicken, cut in serving-size pieces
1	tablespoon vegetable oil
¾	cup orange juice
¼	cup honey
2	chicken bouillon cubes, crumbled
½	teaspoon rosemary
1	3-inch stick cinnamon
½	cup dried apricots
½	cup sliced scallions

In a mixing bowl, mix the flour, salt, garlic powder, and ginger. Roll the chicken pieces in the flour mixture. Heat the oil in a large frying pan and brown the chicken on all sides.

In a mixing bowl, combine the orange juice, honey, bouillon, and rosemary and pour the mixture over the chicken. Add the cinnamon stick, apricots, and scallions and bring everything to a boil. Reduce the heat, cover, and simmer for 25 minutes. Uncover and cook over medium heat for 3 to 5 minutes, spooning the sauce over the chicken frequently until it is glazed. Transfer to a serving dish and serve hot.

Makes 6 servings.

Sesame Chicken

¼ *cup sesame seeds*
2 *tablespoons butter*
2 *tablespoons sesame oil*
1 *small onion, finely chopped*
1 *tablespoon cracked or bulgur wheat*
  Salt and pepper to taste
1 *egg*
1 *tablespoon chopped parsley*
2¼ *pounds chicken*

Brown ⅛ cup of the sesame seeds in a frying pan without any fat, then add 1 tablespoon each of the butter and oil. Add the onion and cracked wheat or bulgur and sauté for 5 minutes, stirring frequently. Remove the pan from heat and stir in a pinch of salt and pepper. Cool slightly, then mix in the egg and parsley.

Preheat the oven to 425°. Stuff the chicken with the wheat mixture and sew up. Mix the remaining sesame seeds with salt and pepper and coat the chicken with this mixture, rubbing it in well.

In a saucepan, heat the remaining oil and butter and brush the chicken with half of the mixture. Place the chicken, breast side down, in a roasting pan. Roast 25 minutes, turn over, and roast for another 25 minutes. Brush with the but-ter-oil mixture and roast for 10 to 15 minutes. Baste the chicken several times with the cooking juices. Turn the oven off and let the dish rest 10 minutes before serving.

Makes 4 to 6 servings.

Orange Beef

3	tablespoons orange marmalade, apricot jam, or pineapple jam, no sugar added
3	tablespoons orange juice concentrate
¼	teaspoon grated ginger root
½	teaspoon fresh lemon juice
2	teaspoons garlic, crushed
¼	teaspoon paprika
1	tablespoon soy sauce
2	to 3 pounds sirloin tips
2	teaspoons cornstarch
1	tablespoon cold water
	Brown rice

In a mixing bowl, combine the jam, orange juice, ginger root, lemon juice, garlic, paprika, and soy sauce and pour the mixture over the beef in a baking dish. Bake, covered with vented foil, at 350° for 30 minutes, basting once.

Drain the juices into a small saucepan and combine them with the cornstarch mixture, cook the mixture until thickened. Serve the beef arranged over brown rice.

Makes 6 servings.

Working at the Truckstop

Raspberry Pork Steaks

4   *pork steaks*
¼   *teaspoon salt*
¼   *teaspoon pepper*
¼   *cup butter, melted*
⅓   *cup chopped onion*
⅓   *cup raspberry vinegar*
⅓   *cup whipping cream*
1   *cup fresh raspberries*
       Fresh mint sprigs for garnish

Sprinkle the pork with salt and pepper. In a skillet fry the steaks in the melted butter for 5 minutes on each side. Remove the pork from the skillet, add the onion, and sauté until it is tender. Replace the pork, add the vinegar, and cook, covered, for 5 minutes. Remove the pork, keep warm.

Reduce the heat to low, add the cream and ¾ cup of the berries, and heat, stirring gently. Spoon the sauce over the pork and top with the remaining berries. Garnish with fresh mint sprigs if desired.

Makes 4 servings.

Lemon Basil Chicken and Vegetables

2   *tablespoons cornstarch*
1   *teaspoon sugar*
1   *cup chicken broth*
½   *teaspoon grated lemon peel*
3   *tablespoons lemon juice*
2   *tablespoons oil*
1   *boneless skinless chicken breast, cut into strips*
1½   *cups sliced zucchini*
1½   *cups sliced yellow squash*
1   *medium red bell pepper, cut into ¼-inch strips (1 cup)*
1   *tablespoon fresh chopped basil or ½ teaspoon dried basil*
8   *ounces fettuccine, cooked, rinsed, and kept warm*

In a mixing bowl, combine the cornstarch and sugar, blending well. Stir in the chicken broth, lemon peel, and lemon juice and set aside.

In a skillet or wok, heat 1 tablespoon of the cooking oil over medium-high heat until hot. Add the chicken and cook until it is tender and no longer pink, about 5 minutes. Remove the chicken and liquid from the skillet and set aside. Heat the remaining oil in the skillet until it is hot and add the zucchini, yellow squash, and red pepper; cook until the vegetables are crisp-tender. Add the cornstarch mixture and chicken and cook until thoroughly heated and slightly thickened, stirring occasionally. Serve over the cooked pasta. Sprinkle with basil.

Makes 4 servings.

Honey Baked Chicken

3	*pounds chicken, cut up*
⅓	*cup butter, melted*
⅓	*cup honey*
2	*tablespoons mustard*
1	*teaspoon salt*
1	*teaspoon curry powder*
	Brown or white rice

Arrange the chicken skin side up, in a 13x9-inch pan. In a small bowl, combine the butter, honey, mustard, salt, and curry powder, and pour the mixture over the chicken. Bake at 350° for 1¼ hours, basting occasionally. Serve with hot cooked rice.

Makes 6 to 8 servings.

Herbed Butter Roasted Chicken

4	to 5 pounds whole roasting chicken
¼	cup butter, softened
1	teaspoon rosemary leaves, crushed
1	teaspoon salt
¼	teaspoon pepper
2	tablespoon chopped fresh parsley
1	teaspoon minced fresh garlic

Preheat the oven to 350°. Secure the wings of the chicken to its body. In a small mixing bowl, stir together the remaining ingredients and rub the chicken with the mixture. Place the chicken on a rack in a roasting pan and roast for 2 to 2½ hours or until fork-tender.

Makes 8 servings.

Coconut Pecan Shrimp

¾	cup cocktail peanuts
2	cups coconut
¼	cup all-purpose flour
2	eggs
2	pounds jumbo shrimp
	Oil for cooking

Dipping Sauce:

3	tablespoons honey
3	tablespoon orange marmalade
1	tablespoon soy sauce
½	teaspoon prepared mustard

In a food processor finely chop the nuts. Combine the chopped nuts and the coconut. Put the flour in a mixing bowl. In another bowl, beat the eggs. Dredge the shrimp in the flour, egg, and nut mixtures, in that order.

Cook the shrimp 6 pieces at a time in ½ inch of hot oil at 350° for 4 to 6 minutes, until they are golden brown, turning once. Drain.

Combine ingredients for the dipping sauce and serve with the shrimp.

Makes 6 to 8 servings.

Creamed Chicken

2	*tablespoons chicken fat*
2	*tablespoons flour*
¼	*teaspoon salt*
1	*cup chicken stock*
1	*cup milk*
2	*cups chicken, cooked*
2	*egg yolks*
¼	*cup cream*
½	*teaspoon lemon juice*
2	*teaspoons parsley*

In a skillet, melt the fat and stir in the flour, salt, chicken stock, and milk. Cook the mixture until it bubbles. Add the chicken to the sauce.

In a small bowl, beat the egg yolks a bit and add the cream. Just before serving, add this mixture to the chicken mixture and cook for 2 minutes. Add the lemon juice and parsley and serve immediately.

Makes 6 servings.

Cinnamon Orange Beef

2	tablespoons all-purpose flour
	Salt and pepper to taste
1	teaspoon ground cinnamon
2	pounds stew beef
4	tablespoons butter
½	cup beef broth
2	oranges

In a small bowl combine the flour, salt, pepper, and cinnamon. Coat the beef with the seasoned flour. In a large frying pan, melt the butter and add the beef; sauté for 20 minutes or until tender and brown all over. Remove the beef and drain it on paper towels. Keep it warm. Pour off the fat from the pan and add the beef broth, finely grated rind, and juice from 1 orange. Bring to a boil, whisking constantly.

Arrange the beef on a serving platter and pour the sauce on top of it. Peel the remaining orange, removing the skin and pith; slice it thinly and arrange on top of the beef.

Makes 4 to 6 servings.

Chicken with Lemon Sauce

½	cup butter
2	broiler chickens, halved
1	clove garlic, crushed
1½	teaspoon salt
¼	cup salad oil
½	cup lemon juice
2	tablespoons minced onion
½	teaspoon pepper
½	teaspoon thyme

In a heavy frying pan with lid, melt the butter. Add the chicken and brown it well on all sides. Combine the remaining ingredients and pour them over the chicken. Cover the pan tightly, and cook over low heat for about 40 minutes or until the chicken is tender. Transfer to a serving dish and serve.

Makes 8 servings.

Chicken with Almonds

¼	cup vegetable oil
2	tablespoons butter
2½	pounds chicken pieces
2	onions, thinly sliced
3	tomatoes, skinned, seeded and chopped
⅛	teaspoon cinnamon
	Salt and pepper to taste
1½	cup chicken broth
5	tablespoon blanched almonds
½	cup seedless golden raisins
4	cups hot rice

Preheat the oven to 375°. In a frying pan, heat the oil and butter. Add the chicken pieces and brown on all sides. Add onions, tomatoes, cinnamon, salt, and pepper. Cook over low heat for 3 to 4 minutes, then transfer to an ovenproof casserole. Add the chicken broth, cover, and cook for 30 minutes. Add the almonds and raisins and cook for 30 more minutes.

Line a large oval platter with hot cooked rice and pile the chicken pieces in the center of the platter. To serve, season the sauce to taste and pour over the chicken.

Makes 6 to 8 servings.

Honey Pork Ribs

½   cup all-purpose flour
1   teaspoon salt
12   country style pork ribs
½   cup butter, melted
¼   cup lemon juice
1   tablespoon soy sauce
½   cup honey

Preheat the oven to 350°. In a shallow pan, combine the flour and salt. Dip the ribs in the flour mixture and arrange them in a baking dish. Pour the melted butter over the ribs and bake for 30 minutes. Mix the remaining ingredients together in a small bowl and pour them over the ribs. Bake for an additional 30 minutes, basting them often. Remove them from the heat and serve them hot. Sometimes I put the ribs on the grill for 10 minutes after I remove them from the oven.
Makes 4 servings.

Lime Barbecue Chicken

1   to 2 pounds chicken pieces, skinned
1   cup ketchup with onion
⅓   cup fresh lime juice
1   lime sliced

Place the chicken in a lightly greased 13x9-inch baking dish. In a small mixing bowl, combine the ketchup and fresh lime juice and pour it over the chicken. Top with lime slices and bake at 350° for 45 minutes.
Makes 4 servings.

Grilled Ginger Glazed Chicken

¼   cup Dijon mustard
2   tablespoons brown sugar
2   tablespoons honey
2   teaspoons peeled, minced, fresh ginger
8   chicken breast halves, skinned and boned
     Garnish: fresh parsley sprigs

Combine the Dijon mustard, brown sugar, honey, and ginger in a small bowl. Place the chicken breasts in a lightly greased 11x7-inch baking dish and brush the mustard mixture over the chicken. Bake at 375° for 15 minutes or until done, then broil them 4 inches from heat (with electric oven door partially open) for 1 to 2 minutes or until golden

Coat a food rack with vegetable cooking spray and place it on a grill over medium-high heat (350 to 400°). Place the chicken on the rack and brush it with half of the mustard mixture. Grill for 5 minutes, turn the chicken over, and brush with the remaining mustard mixture. Grill for 5 more minutes or until done. Garnish, if desired.
Makes 8 servings.

With David Foster

Pecan Chicken

4   chicken breast halves, skinned and boned
2   tablespoons honey
2   tablespoons Dijon mustard
2   tablespoons finely chopped pecans

Place chicken breasts between two sheets of heavy-duty plastic wrap and flatten them to a thickness of ¼-inch using a meat mallet or rolling pan. In a small bowl, combine the honey and Dijon mustard, spread the mixture on both sides of the chicken and dredge in the pecans. Arrange the breasts in a lightly greased 8-inch-square baking dish, and bake at 350° for 15 to 18 minutes or until done.
Makes 4 servings.

Buttermilk Chicken

¾   cup grated Parmesan cheese
¾   cup finely crushed corn flakes cereal
1   envelope buttermilk dressing mix
6   chicken breast halves, skinned
½   cup butter or margarine, melted

In a small bowl, combine the Parmesan cheese, corn flakes, and buttermilk dressing mix. Dip the chicken in the melted butter and dredge in the cereal mixture. Place the chicken in a lightly greased 13x9-inch baking dish and bake at 350° for 45 to 50 minutes or until done.
Makes 6 servings.

Citrus-Dijon Chicken and Rice

1	2-pound whole chicken
2	tablespoons all-purpose flour
1	large size oven bag
¾	cup orange juice
¼	cup Dijon mustard
¾	cup water
1	cup uncooked long-grain rice
2	tablespoons brown sugar

Cut the chicken into desired pieces and remove the skin. Add flour to the oven bag, twist the end of the bag, and shake. Add the orange juice, mustard, water, rice, and brown sugar and squeeze the bag to blend the ingredients. Place the oven bag in a 13x9-inch baking dish. Add the chicken to the bag, turn the bag to coat the chicken with the sauce, and arrange the chicken pieces in a single layer. Close the bag with a nylon tie, cut 6½-inch slits in the top of bag, and bake the chicken mixture at 350° for 45 minutes or until the chicken is done.

Makes 4 to 6 servings.

Gaylord Sartain and Damon resting on the set

Sesame-Parmesan Chicken

1   cup all-purpose flour
1   cup soft breadcrumbs
½   cup sesame seeds
2   teaspoons seasoned salt
1   teaspoon pepper
1   cup grated Parmesan cheese
3   pounds chicken thighs
1   8-ounce bottle Italian dressing

In a large heavy-duty zip-top plastic bag combine the flour, breadcrumbs, sesame seeds, seasoned salt, pepper, and Parmesan cheese. Dip half of the chicken thighs in the Italian dressing, place in the bag, and shake gently. Place the coated chicken on a lightly greased 15x10-inch jellyroll pan. Repeat the procedure with the remaining chicken. Bake at 375° for 50 minutes or until done.

Makes 6 to 8 servings.

The Culhanes

Sautéed Chicken and Nectarines with Linguini

3   small nectarines, rinsed
6   ounces linguini, cooked and drained
8   ounces boneless, skinless chicken breast
    Salt and pepper to taste
2   tablespoons olive oil
1   cup chopped green onions
⅓   cup chicken stock
¼   cup dry white wine
4   tablespoon cold butter, cut into cubes
    Fresh herbs or parsley and lemon for garnish

Halve and pit the nectarines. Cut them into wedges, and set them aside. Cook the linguini according to the package directions. Drain and keep warm.

While the linguini is cooking, cut the chicken pieces into bite-size pieces and season with salt and pepper. In a 10-inch sauté pan, heat the oil over medium-high heat. Add the chicken and cook for approximately 5 minutes until done. Add the nectarines and onions and sauté for 2 minutes, stirring gently. Deglaze the pan with the chicken stock and wine, bring to a boil, and whisk in the butter to thicken the sauce. To serve, divide the cooked linguini onto 2 serving plates and spoon the chicken and nectarine wedges over it. Garnish with fresh herbs and lemon wedges.

Makes 2 servings.

Herb Crusted Roasted Salmon

2	*tablespoon chopped shallots*
1	*tablespoon tamarind paste or 3 pods*
1	*cup white wine*
¼	*cup rice vinegar*
1	*cup water*
2	*cup cream*
6	*tablespoon olive oil*
2	*cup chopped chives*
	Fresh ground pepper
4	*large salmon filets*

In a heavy saucepan, place the chopped shallots, tamarind, vinegar, wine, and water. Bring to a boil and let it reduce to ¼ cup liquid. Add the cream and reduce by ¼ or to the desired consistency. Season with salt and pepper and set it aside until ready to serve.

Preheat the oven to 450°. In a mixing bowl, combine the olive oil, chives, and fresh ground pepper, and coat the fish on both sides. Place the salmon on a jellyroll pan, set in the upper part of the preheated oven, and bake for 5 minutes. Turn the oven down to 350° and bake for another 5 minutes. Check for doneness: the fish should flake easily with a fork. To serve, place a little sauce on the plate and place the fish on top of it. Lace with a little more sauce.

Makes 4 servings.

Sweet and Sour Meatballs

Apricot Glaze:
¼   cup oil
¼   cup vinegar or lemon juice
⅓   cup catsup
½   teaspoon salt
½   cup apricot jam
2   tablespoon brown sugar
¼   to ½ cup grated onion
½   teaspoon oregano

Meatballs:
5   eggs
½   cup cottage cheese
1   cup walnuts, ground into meal
½   teaspoon salt
1   cup cubed whole wheat bread
1   cup shredded Cheddar cheese
½   cup finely chopped onion
1   teaspoon crushed basil
½   teaspoon sage
1   cup herb stuffing

Combine the apricot glaze ingredients in a saucepan on medium heat. Once they are blended and the mixture bubbles, simmer on low heat for 15 minutes.

Mix all of the meatball ingredients together and shape into 25 small balls. Place in a 9x13-inch dish.

Pour the apricot glaze over the balls and bake in the oven at 350° for 30 to 35 minutes.

Makes 25 meatballs.

Chicken Crunch

I know it may sound odd to use Cap'n Crunch cereal for dinner, but this dish is soooo scrumptious!

1	cup Cap'n Crunch Cereal
1	cup corn flakes
1	cup all-purpose flour
1	tablespoon granulated onion
1	tablespoon garlic
2	teaspoon ground black pepper
2	eggs
1	cup milk
8	chicken tenderloins or breast cut into strips

In a blender pulse the Cap'n Crunch and corn flakes until the mixture is the consistency of fine crumbs, and pour it into a mixing bowl. In a second bowl combine the flour, onion, garlic, and pepper.

Beat the eggs and mix it with the milk in yet another bowl. Dredge the breast tenderloins first in the milk mixture, then in the flour mixture, and finally in the cereal crumbs. Deep fry at 325° for 3 to 4 minutes or until cooked thoroughly. Serve with Creole mustard.

Makes 8 servings.

Apricot Chicken for Two

8	ounces boneless, skinless chicken breast
¼	cup apricot preserves
¼	cup dry white wine or white wine vinegar
	ground white pepper to taste
¼	clove fresh garlic

Cut the chicken into julienne strips and sauté in a skillet using vegetable cooking spray. After cooking the chicken thoroughly, remove it from the skillet, but keep it warm in a separate dish. Place the apricot preserves, white pepper, and garlic in the skillet and simmer for 3 minutes. Add the chicken to the mixture and simmer for 1 minute. Serve over rice of choice.

Makes 2 servings.

Pasta Shells With Greens and Beans

½   *cup fresh tomato basil sauce*
1   *package fresh spinach*
4   *slices bacon, chopped*
3   *cloves garlic, minced*
1   *small onion, chopped*
1   *can white beans, drained and rinsed*
1   *pound shell pasta, cooked and drained*

In a medium saucepan, heat the tomato basil sauce thoroughly and set aside. Thoroughly wash the spinach in cold water, remove and discard the stems. Tear the spinach leaves coarsely and set aside.

In a large skillet, cook the bacon until it is crisp and drain the fat. In the same skillet, sauté the garlic and onion until it is tender. Add the beans and cook the mixture over low heat until it is heated through, stirring occasionally. Add the spinach to the skillet, cover, and cook just until spinach is wilted. Toss the cooked pasta with the heated sauce and top with the spinach and bean mixture, lightly toss to coat.

Makes 6 servings.

Smoked Salmon in Puffed Pastry

This sounds and tastes very elegant, but only takes minutes to prepare.

2   *tablespoon unsalted butter*
1   *cup heavy cream*
2   *leeks, white only, sliced and cleaned*
1   *pound smoked salmon*
2   *sheets puff pastry*
2   *egg yolks, beaten*
       Salt, pepper, and nutmeg to taste

In a small skillet, sauté the leeks in butter and cream over medium-high heat with salt, pepper, and nutmeg. Drain excess moisture.

Preheat the oven to 450°. Roll out half the pastry to a 25 x 6-inch rectangle, ¼ inch thick. Cover the pastry with leeks, leaving a narrow border around the edges. Place the smoked fish on top of the leeks. Roll out second strip of puff pastry slightly larger than the first. Brush the edge of the bottom strip of pastry with egg yolk and place over the fish, sealing the edges. Bake for 12 minutes. Trim the edges and cut in diagonals into 4 portions.

Makes 4 servings.

Tomato Onion Relish

This goes over pork tenderloins or chicken, and it is out of this world, honey.

¼   *cup golden raisins*
¼   *cup Jack Daniel's Tennessee Whiskey (optional)*
3   *large onions, coarsely chopped*
2   *tablespoons oil*
1   *tablespoon brown sugar*
1   *14½-ounce can chopped tomatoes, drained*

½   teaspoon thyme
       Black pepper and salt to taste

In a small bowl, combine the raisins and Jack Daniel's and set aside to soak. In a large skillet, heat the oil. Add the onions, cover, and cook over low heat until the onions are tender and begin to caramelize, about 15 minutes, stirring occasionally. Uncover the skillet and stir in the brown sugar and continue cooking for 5 minutes. Stir in the tomatoes, raisins, and Jack Daniel's. Increase the heat and bring the mixture to a boil. Reduce the heat and simmer for 10 minutes or until thickened. Season with thyme, pepper, and salt. Cool and refrigerate. Serve chilled or at room temperature.
       Makes 10 to 12 servings.

Oven BBQ Tennessee Pork Tenderloin

¼   *cup Jack Daniel's Tennessee Whiskey (Optional)*
¼   *cup soy sauce*
¼   *cup catsup*
½   *cup packed brown sugar*
½   *teaspoon garlic powder*
5   *pounds pork tenderloins*

Preheat the oven to 450°. In a small saucepan, combine the whiskey, soy sauce, catsup, brown sugar, and garlic. Bring the mixture to a boil and simmer until it is slightly thickened, about 5 minutes. This sauce is sticky, so line a baking or roasting pan with foil for easy clean up.
       Place the tenderloins in a foil-lined pan and brush with the sauce. Roast for about 30 minutes (until internal temperature is 155° to 160°). Remove them from the oven and let them rest at least 15 minutes before slicing.
       Makes 12 servings.

Lulu's Nashville Fried Catfish and Yummy Fried Pickles

If you want a taste of the real south, honey, you gotta fix yourself these delicious recipes.

Fried Catfish:

1	cup all-purpose flour
1	teaspoon seasoning mix
½	cup yellow cornmeal
½	cup white cornmeal
2	large eggs
½	cup milk
6	catfish fillets
1	teaspoon salt
1	cup vegetable oil
	Seasoning Mix (recipe follows)

In a shallow dish, combine the all purpose flour and seasonings. In a second dish, combine the yellow cornmeal and white cornmeal. In a third dish or bowl, beat the eggs and milk. Season the catfish fillets with the salt. Dredge the catfish one at a time first in the flour, then the egg wash, and then the cornmeal, shaking to remove any excess.

In a deep cast-iron skillet, heat the vegetable oil and fry the fish in batches, cooking them until golden brown on 1 side, 4 to 5 minutes. Turn over and cook until golden brown on the second side and completely cooked through, 4 to 5 minutes. Remove the fillets and drain them on paper towels. Season lightly with the Seasoning Mix. Add 1 cup vegetable oil as needed to cook the remaining fish.

Makes 6 servings.

Seasoning Mix:

2	tablespoons salt
2½	tablespoons paprika
2	tablespoons garlic powder

1   *tablespoons black pepper*
1   *tablespoon onion powder*
1   *tablespoon cayenne pepper*
1   *tablespoon dried oregano leaf*
1   *tablespoon dried thyme.*

Combine all of the seasonings in a shallow dish and stir until thoroughly mixed.

Fried Pickles:
1   *16-ounce jar dill pickles*
1   *cup buttermilk*
2   *tablespoons hot red pepper sauce*
1   *cup all-purpose flour*
1   *cup cornmeal*
2   *tablespoons Seasoning Mix (see recipe, above)*
4   *cups vegetable oil*
     Salt to taste

Drain the jar of sliced dill pickles in a colander, then spread them on paper towels to drain completely. Combine the buttermilk and hot red pepper sauce (optional) in a bowl. In a separate bowl, combine the flour, cornmeal, and seasoning mix.

   In a medium size pot, heat the vegetable oil to 350°. Submerge the pickles in batches in the buttermilk, then dip them into the flour mixture, tossing to coat evenly. Shake them in a strainer to remove any excess batter and add them to the oil in batches, turning until golden brown and crisp, about 2 minutes. Drain the pickles on paper towels and season them with the Seasoning Mix and salt. Serve them hot. They are great when dipped in Ranch or Blue Cheese dressing, too!
   Makes 6 servings.

LuLu's Hush Puppies Jalapeño

1½   *cups yellow cornmeal*
½   *cup bleached all-purpose flour*
1   *teaspoon baking powder*
1   *teaspoon salt*
1   *teaspoon hot sauce (use your favorite brand)*
¼   *cup minced yellow onion*
2   *fresh jalapeños, seeded and minced*
2   *large eggs, beaten*
½   *cup milk*
4   *cups vegetable oil*
      Seasonings to taste (paprika, salt, garlic powder, cayenne
      pepper, thyme, onion powder, black pepper, dried oregano
      leaf)

In a large bowl, combine the cornmeal, flour, baking powder, salt, hot sauce, onion, and jalapeños, and mix well. Add the eggs and milk and stir to make the batter.

In a large pot, heat the oil to 360°. Drop in the batter one heaping teaspoon at a time in batches of 5 or 6. When the hush puppies rise to the surface of the pot, roll them around in the oil with a slotted spoon to brown them evenly on all sides. Remove and drain them on a paper-lined plate and season to taste while they are still hot.

Makes 6 servings.

Pan Seared Atlantic Salmon

1	tablespoon olive oil
6	ounces salmon
2	tablespoons butter
¼	cup sliced Morel mushrooms
¼	cup sliced Shitake mushrooms
¼	cup sliced Chanterelle mushrooms
¼	cup sliced Portabella mushrooms
2	tablespoons diced shallots
¼	cup Madeira wine
1	cup heavy cream
4	potatoes
1	tablespoon minced garlic
2	tablespoons sour cream
	salt and pepper to taste
2	cups fried leeks

In a skillet heat the olive oil and sauté the salmon until it reaches the desired temperature. Take it out of the pan and place it in a warm oven until ready to serve.

Add the butter to the pan and heat until melted. Sauté the mushrooms and shallots until they are tender. Add the Madeira and cook for 1 minute. Add the heavy cream and cook the sauce until it is thick.

In a stock pot boil the potatoes until they are tender and drain off the water. In a mixer combine the potatoes, garlic, sour cream, salt, and pepper.

To serve, place the potato mixture in the center of each plate, top with the salmon, and pour the mushroom sauce over the salmon. Garnish with fried leeks.

Makes 2 servings.

Forever Lasting Love

The first time I touched him he was ten days old. I couldn't hold him. I could only touch his little hands, stroke his beautiful little face, and cry. I cried because I wanted him to be mine. I wanted to snatch him up from that hospital bed, pull those tubes and needles from his thin little body, and wrap him up and run. He was astonishingly beautiful. He looked like a real-life cherub; many thought he was a girl.

He should have been a healthy baby boy, but his mother was a drug abuser. He had something called acute respiratory syndrome, his lungs full of fluid caused by side effects of the amphetamines his mother had continued to use through her pregnancy.

I left the hospital that day angry, confused, and hopeless. My heart had somehow started to come to life, looking at that beautiful little boy, wanting to take him away from all that pain and his struggle to breathe, to live.

I remembered someone in my past saying that God loved me so much He gave His Son for my life. Now all I wanted was for Him to give life to my son. Yes, he was mine. He was still clinging to life after ten days of struggle, and it was all my fault.

His name was Damon Erik, and he was my only hope in the life of pain I was sentenced to. I prayed the day he was born, for the first time in my life that I could remember. Before, my pain and rage were of such magnitude that I didn't want anything to do with a God who dumped on people like me. Now it looked as if He would be my only hope.

I'd never hoped before, never dreamed, never allowed myself to believe I had the right to do anything. I believed I was the unlovable one and would never deserve any good thing. Then here was this beautiful little life, and I was responsible for what was happening to him. The doctor told me they had done everything they knew to do, and now it was up to God to make him better. In the next few days, God did a miraculous thing: He healed my child. The doctors were happy and a bit confused; there was no medical explanation, just no symptoms! I was ecstatic.

I watched them remove the needles and tubes from his small body, and then I got to wrap him up and take him home. Damon was six months old when I gave my heart to Jesus. God had heard my prayer and healed my child before I ever asked Jesus into my heart.

Today, Damon is a grown man in his thirties, and he is still as beautiful as he was that day I first laid eyes on him. He has grown into a remarkable young man with a heart full of love and compassion for a terribly confused, angry young mother who couldn't see past her own pain. His words to me throughout his life have given me the courage to continue on my road to wellness. He still says today, "Mom, I'm so glad God let you be my mother." Words of life to my soul! Words of "Forever Lasting Love."

He Touched Me

Jesus was restoring life and healing to all who had been overpowered by Satan. He was proving that the kingdom of God was now on earth in His very presence. A leper came to Him and said, "If You are willing, You can make me clean." Then Jesus, touched with compassion, said, "I am willing." He touched the leper, who immediately was healed.

There wasn't any question in the leper's mind about Jesus' ability to heal him. The only question he had was whether Jesus would want to heal him. That's true of most of us. We don't question whether Jesus is able to save us, heal us, or bless us.

The question we have is whether He wants to heal us. We know ourselves, and we have voted against ourselves so many times that we project that vote onto the Lord. We assume He would say no, too. Sometimes we don't even bother to ask Jesus to help us. One of the most important things about the leper's story is that Jesus touched him. Lepers were expelled from the community because they were a threat to the well-being of society. This man took considerable risk in leaving the leper colony to go to Jesus, kneel before Him, and say, "If You are willing, You can make me clean." Jesus was moved with compassion.

I've heard the word *compassion* means "two emotions simultaneously working inside the human spirit." The first emotion is one of great love, great empathy, great sorrow, great desire; the other emotion is one of intense anger. Absolute, intolerable rage at what has caused this person's affliction. Regardless of the moment, regardless of what would happen to Him, Jesus was filled with compassion and reached forth His hand to touch the leper. Immediately, the man was healed.

He Was There All the Time

It was the spring of 1985. I was up for a Dove Award and was to sing and be a presenter for the show that year. My lifelong friend Jeanne Tatum was handling some bookings for me, and we traveled together to Nashville. It was the first year the Dove Awards show was held at the Grand Ole Opry.

We traveled from Texas and arrived for rehearsal on the day before the show. We were told there would be two rooms at the hotel for us, and we were rather unhappy to learn they had booked only one. We had to stay in the same room. We are so different. She prefers mild temperatures; I need "icebox" temperatures because I have asthma and allergies, and the cold keeps infection away and aids my breathing. I was wrestling with a case of nerves and an upset stomach, and I decided to take some prescribed medication to calm both.

As I prepared to go to bed, I felt rather itchy and flushed but tried to shake it off and go to sleep. For hours I tried to rest but couldn't. I finally got up as quietly as I could, so as not to wake Jeanne, and went into the bathroom. By then I was having great difficulty breathing as well, and when I looked in the mirror I almost fainted. I was covered in an ugly red rash, and my face, arms, and legs were really swelling! I called out to Jeanne, and she came into the bathroom and immediately called paramedics.

They rushed me to Baptist Hospital, where I spent the night with intravenous medications being pumped into my body to counteract the bad reaction I'd had to the drugs. The doctors told Jeanne that if I had waited any longer, I would have died within a few hours.

I was upset because I didn't want to disappoint the Gospel Music Association by not showing up for the planned events of the next day. Jeanne prayed continuously throughout the night and into the following day. She stayed right there with me in the emergency room all night. Finally, after hours of begging them to release me, they allowed me to go back to the hotel the next morning. Jeanne helped with my makeup and hair and dressing for the day's rehearsals and the show that evening.

She has been an angel in my life on many occasions. I believe her prayers got me through those two days. I was able to do all I was asked to do. I had the honor and privilege of singing "The King of Who I Am" with my precious friend Russ Taff. The song was on my album titled *You Were Loving Me*. I won the coveted Dove Award that year. I've never been too concerned about winning awards, mostly because I don't cater to the politics that accompany so many of them, but I was pleasantly surprised and, I must say, excited, to win that one.

I think back to that time and am humbled at how God was there in the midst of the situation. So many times, I have questioned His presence, and He later reminds me that He was there all the time! If I would only open my spiritual vision to see Him there, I could be at peace in every situation. I stand amazed at His constant ability to "stay" when we are the ones who move away from Him; having taken our eyes off Him. I am so thankful for His patience as I continue to work on my vision. It is such a blessing to look back and know "He was there all the time."

Prelude

I don't have vivid memories of certain times in my life, although the memories I do have are pungent and profound. In this picture of my life, I will draw from the well of God's love to bring to mind those things that will exalt Him and hopefully cause you to reflect on His grace in your own life. I believe He has called me to be a public witness for His cause: your heart.

I also believe He is the only true answer to every question, doubt, pain, and situation you will encounter in your life. Having subjected myself to every kind of pain and empty promise this world has to offer, I am once again starting over. After many trys, I again whisper His name. I again covet His mercy. Through yet more of His lessons of grace, I again try to become more like Him.

As you read these pages of one life struggling to be accepted, begging to be wanted and belong, remember: You and I are His precious children—the twinkle in His eyes, the beat of His heart, and the very essence of life to Him. He has created us to walk with Him, to talk with Him, and to bring life to His Spirit with our praise.

Allow Him to teach you who you are in Him. Every day He will change you, if you will allow Him. Every day He will give meaning to life's unfairness with hope, mercy, and grace, the very fuel that keeps hearts afire. Let Him enfold your heart with His breath, the breath of life.

Slain in The Spirit

In the spring of 1973, I was invited to California to give my testimony on *The Kathryn Kuhlman Show*. I was a baby Christian and knew only what I had heard or seen briefly on some TV news coverage about Miss Kuhlman. I asked my friend Diane to accompany me since it was a new experience. I didn't even know what a testimony was.

Diane explained that a testimony was simply telling the story of what God had done for me in my troubled life. I just jumped into it headfirst and was ready to tell every detail. Diane spent hours laughing at me, saying, "Lu, you can't tell that!" With much love and correction, she helped me decide what to tell and what not to tell.

I was raised in a strict Baptist environment and had no education of the Spirit-filled life. I was skeptical, to say the least. After a bit of encouragement from my friend, I agreed to go on one condition, that Kathryn would not touch me. I had seen people "slain in the Spirit," and it scared me. I thought people were being knocked out. I didn't want anything to do with that.

When we arrived in California, we were taken to the studio where Kathryn did her program. Everyone on staff was kind and accommodating. When Kathryn entered the room, it was like a sweet fragrance encompassed the entire area. I quickly noticed she was very different from anyone I'd ever met. Her speech was slow and emphatic.

She was earnest and sincere in her desire to get my testimony of God's grace out to the television audience. I sang a couple of songs, and I was then escorted to the table where she was sitting. She sat at a round table across from me. I liked this arrangement right away because I would be more than an arm's length from her. As I began to tell of the years of abandonment and the deep hurt of not knowing any kind of acceptance, she began to weep.

I told stories of my years of drug abuse and my desire to commit suicide at every turn. She was so moved with compassion. I continued to tell of how God had watched me and covered me and protected my steps even when I didn't acknowledge Him. I told how He had spared me from prison and given me a desire to be a servant in His kingdom all the days of my life.

Before we could get to the end of the program, something remarkable happened. Kathryn was "slain in the Spirit." Her eyes closed, her head went down, and she was just out. I didn't know what to do, so I just sat there with my mouth hanging open. Quickly, Diane and I were ushered into a small theater next to the studio.

In a few moments Miss Kuhlman and her assistant came into the theater, and we all watched the day's segments together. While we watched, she was so sweet and talked like we had known each other for a lifetime. As we were preparing to leave, she came in and asked where Diane was. She hugged her and prayed with her. She wanted to know this wonderful person who had loved me and was directly responsible for my change.

After her time with Diane, we were told it was very rare for Miss Kuhlman to come out to talk to anyone who was not on the program. It was such a special occasion for us. It would take me years to realize that in our times of fear, God is tender and touched with our weaknesses. He showed me something so beautiful in meeting Kathryn Kuhlman. We can always rest in the unexpected when it is God's appointed time for a new experience or lesson. He will never embarrass us or humiliate us when He is working His plan.

Junior Sample

He was exactly what you saw! In fact, his motto was: "What you see is what you get." His name was Junior Samples, and he was *Hee Haw's* very own authentic "country boy."

The story, as told to me, was that they literally found him walking down a street in Georgia carrying his fishing gear and asked him if he would like to be on television, and he said something like, "Well, I reckon." He was a true example of pure country. When we first found him, he was completely illiterate. Before he left us, he had become "dumb like a fox."

My friend, the infamous Junior Samples

He was a sweet man with health problems, some self-inflicted but others genetic. The first time I met him, I couldn't believe he was real. He was so pure in everything he did. There were no hidden agendas. Junior was simply Junior. He made me laugh until my body ached. He made everyone laugh. The studio was filled with hilarious laughter for hours at a time because of him.

After a few years, he determined he wanted to learn to read and write, which he did well. So after that they made it a game to find every five-syllable word that could trip him up and just let him go.

He was so funny, people would stay for hours after their release for the day just to watch him. When he was in truly bad health, the last time we were filming before he left us, he said, "LuLu, I ain't gonna be here long." He was weak and tired of fighting all the health problems.

I said, "In that case, Junior, can I ask you a question? Has anyone ever told you about Jesus?" His eyes started to tear up, and he said, "LuLu, I could show you the rock I was sitting on when the Lord saved me." I almost fell out of the rocking chair I was sitting in.

Sometime earlier, he had made a commitment to God. He wanted to build each of his six children a home before he passed and promised his heart to God if he would be permitted to complete his task. I believe he did build those homes for his children, with his own hands. And I believe he gave his life to the Lord.

Junior's pastor gave me the privilege of singing "Amazing Grace" at his homegoing celebration. He taught many lessons to all of us in the *Hee Haw* family—lessons of courage and determination, as well as lessons of how laughter can heal the soul. He had bad days as well as good days, as do we all, but overall his presence made our lives a little bit lighter when the days were too long or the cornfields were too tall.

I thank the good Lord for the experience of knowing Junior and his wife, Grace, and their children. They were inspirations to me, and I know they were as proud of him as the cast of the show was. The thing I am most proud of is knowing I will see him again.

Healing in Truth

I moved to Nashville in 1991, with my two boys, SiSi the dog, and several overloaded trucks and cars in tow. It was quite a sight to see. I had lost my very expensive home with the forty-foot swimming pool I had always dreamed of and the life I had hoped would complete the perfect story. I've had to start over several times in my life because of choices I made that were based on my neediness and unstable state of mind. I knew my life would change again. I just never thought it would change to the degree it has.

With the help and love of friends, I was directed to a wonderful Christian counselor. His name is Dee White. He and his wife, Barbara, are marriage and relationship counselors. Dee was gracious to take me into his counsel, and I will always be grateful for his steadfast love and truth to my life. At first I was terrified to think I had to allow anyone into my troubled mind and heart. It is very scary to open up and spill pieces of a broken heart all over someone you don't know. He was so patient with me. He never once acted as if he were looking down on me or judging me. He simply and quietly asked questions that hit me like a steamroller.

On one occasion, he asked me a simple question, and I was dumbfounded to think I'd never thought of it myself. His question was, "What if fat is not an issue with God?" It made be burst into tears, because I have judged myself the way society has taught me to judge others all my life. It is the one thing I have hated myself for every minute of every day. Why wouldn't God judge me for being fat, too?

My self-worth was based on what I looked like and what narrow-minded, prejudiced people had made me believe was the "set in stone" standard of acceptance. All my life, my identity has been based on what others think when they look at me. I have done everything I could to change my size. I have tried so many diets I should be a "diet consultant" by now. I have eaten such horrible food I should have lost my whole body weight, and even had major surgery more than once to make myself acceptable by society's standards. It gained me nothing but self-loathing and one angry spirit that wanted to lash out at "stupidity."

Needless to say, his questions set me on a new road to wellness and acceptance of myself based on what God thinks of me and not what hurtful people say. In the last eleven years, I have moved from self-hatred, feeling unworthy of anyone's love and striving to meet worldly standards, to learning who I am in Jesus. Although there are still days I can't manage to see past the pain of being "looked down on" and "unaccepted," I am moving into the truth of how He sees me, and that is all-important to me now. I still find myself alone most of the time, but I am learning to spend quality time with

God, and He is showing me that fat is not an issue with Him.

Dee asked me one more of those earth-shaking questions at the end of our two years of working together: "What if God designed you to look the way you do, as a blessing to your life?" I screamed, "Oh, great! You mean He gave me this curse as a blessing?" I wanted to throw up! Dee then said, "How many people do you know who look like you and can stand and tell other hurting people that there is healing for their pain in a God who doesn't look at the flesh you wear, but at your heart?" This way of thinking was a revelation to my life and changed me more than any other thing I have learned.

This world, with all its pain and prejudice, will pass away. God does not judge us by our appearance. It doesn't matter to Him if we are fat or thin, tall or short, black or white, brown or yellow. He doesn't want our body; He wants our heart, and that is all that matters. Each day I strive to give Him more of my heart, and my eyes look only to Him, for He is the One who paid the ultimate price. When Jesus went to the cross, He accepted you and me. More than that, He approved of us! I grow in this knowledge more every day.

Cookies

They come in all sizes, shapes, and fabulous flavors. Some are creamy, some are crunchy, and all are yummy. They're a part of some of life's grandest moments. I particularly love pinwheels, a graham cracker cookie topped with marshmallow and covered in rich chocolate.

I also love oatmeal raisin, peanut butter, and lemon cookies. They seem to make life's little hurts more bearable. They soothe children's scrapes and scratches and give a refreshing lift to a long day. I think they make us more tolerable. Sometimes they even make us forget what the "fuss" was all about. They're mediators, you know!

In my life, cookies have been the reconciler in many battles. They make me think of how sweet our Mediator is. Jesus is the flavor of healing, the creamy smoothness of grace, and the refreshing lift of mercy. I look forward to one day, perhaps, having milk and cookies with Him, in person. Yum!

Heaven's Watchin'

Living in Nashville, with all the music that is birthed here, you just might find yourself with a house full of musicians and lots of singing going on. It was on one such occasion that my friend Rebecca from Abundant Life Church came to my home with a young man named Michael Wells. He was tall with dark olive skin, black curly hair, and beautiful brown eyes. He played his guitar and sang, and everyone in the whole house just "blubbered" over him.

Rebecca asked him to sing a song he'd written called "St. Valentines," and we fell all over ourselves. It was so romantic, and he had such an incredible voice, it took us all by surprise.

In the 1970s, a man named Harry Nilsson made a story record called The Point that I used to play for my children. I loved his voice and his music, and I still do today. Michael's voice reminded me of Nilsson's, so, of course, I fell in love with Michael's voice and music.

In the months that followed, we became very good friends. I learned that Michael had come to Nashville from New Jersey to work on a project he'd written. I even rented a room to him in my home for several months. He was so open to being my friend and truly didn't ask me for anything other than friendship. We became very close. We loved to sit on the porch and sing and just enjoy the beautiful days and nights of Tennessee.

He had never really heard my story, and I began to tell him of my life as the days went by. We laughed, cried, and had some wonderful moments just loving God and praising Him.

One day he told me a story. He told me that when he was eight years old, he and his parents were home watching television when they came upon Hee Haw. There was a big lady singing, "Blessed Assurance, Jesus Is Mine." He said that in his spirit the Lord told him that lady would someday have something to do with his music. I almost fell off the porch when he told me his story. I think my eyes must have looked like they would fall out of their sockets. I realized I was that lady, and here he was in my home, telling me about that night the Lord spoke to him almost thirty years ago.

Michael has written some of the best songs I have ever heard or sung. After hearing my stories of how God has watched over me and covered me and carried me throughout my life, he wrote some incredible songs for me. The first of Michael's songs I performed, "Heaven's Watchin'," is on the Intimate Expressions album I did in 1998. It is one of the best songs I've ever done, and people must agree with me because they all want to purchase it after my concerts.

Michael has an anointed way of getting truth into musical notes and sending them out with a powerful awakening. I am so impressed with his talent and love for the Lord that I am going to do a duet with him on my next project, and I plan to do many, many more of his songs. I want the world to know this precious brother and friend and the talents God has given to lift Him up.

I just love God's way of making music and bringing wonderful friends into our lives at the same time! Therefore, it is with a grateful heart I can say the words Michael has written for me:

Heaven's watchin' me
God is on my side
Angels guarding me
Faith can turn the tide
It's no coincidence
Life's no roll of the dice
Someone prayed and now I'm saved
Heaven's watchin' me.

My friend, heaven's watchin' you, too. Think about it!

Chocolate Cake

My youngest son, Justin, was about four years old when he received his first lesson in how important it is to tell the truth. We were all spending precious family time in the pool on a hot day when my little "sneak" announced that he had to go inside to the bathroom.

I had baked a fabulous chocolate cake a couple of days earlier, and there was one piece left. I knew exactly what he would do; yes, he made a beeline for that cake. I got out of the pool and quietly slipped into the house. There he stood in the middle of the kitchen. When I saw him I wanted to burst into hysterical laughter, but I knew he would have to be dealt with.

I turned away just long enough to catch my breath and put on my "stern" face. "Justin Collin," I said, "I thought I told you not to get into that cake!" His eyes were as big as saucers, feet frozen to the floor and a look of horror on his little face. Caught, he had to think fast. He blinked those baby blues and gulped out, "Mama, I didn't." I choked back my laughter again and said, "Justin, don't lie to me." He held his ground like a Ninja Turtle, caught his breath, and mumbled, "Mama, I didn't."

Me and my cute baby boys!

I took his chubby little hand and led him to the bathroom, turned on the light, and stood him on the counter, directly in front of the mirror. His eyes grew big and round as he stared at his reflection. There was chocolate on his nose, chocolate on his cheeks and hands, chocolate in his hair and all around his mouth. He looked like he had just had a fight with Willy Wonka and lost.

The noise that then came from that little body was "piercing," to say the least. It was somewhere between a train whistle and thunder. He moaned and screamed as if he was never again going to eat chocolate cake. I couldn't hold it any longer. I literally dropped to the floor laughing. I laughed until I cried. Justin didn't know whether to laugh or run. He just stood on that counter, tears flowing, covered in chocolate, looking like it was the end of his little world.

It was so funny, I couldn't punish him, so I gently began to wash away all the "evidence" and explain to him that the truth is always less painful than a lie. It took several years to make that a reality in Justin's life. He was always headstrong. Hmm . . . wonder where he got that from?

I am so thankful that the Word of God is a light unto my path. That light is truth, and it will always win. There have been many times in my life when only the truth would bring the hope of life to my wounded soul. Jesus lovingly and gently washed away all the stains of my sin. I still hold my young men to that standard when they ask what to do in life situations. They have honored me by displaying honesty, one of the greatest treasures they possess. I adore them. They are honestly the greatest treasures of my world.

Kenny Price

Kenny Price was bigger than life. He was one of the funniest people I've ever known. When he entered a room, everyone knew he was there. Sometimes his laugh would precede his presence, and you would find yourself waiting to see who this "spirit lifter" was. He commanded attention and could make you laugh when you were in the depths of depression and had no intention of submitting to anything funny. I don't remember one day of my life when he was around that he didn't keep me in stitches.

His music was big and his smile was big, but his heart was huge. He seemed to know how to lift you from dark places into the healing of bright laughter. I remember many days he would have the whole studio laughing so hard we would have to stop and catch our breath before we could continue with our work. He was one of those rare people who could bring your heart to healing with just his words.

We spent many wonderful days together on the *Hee Haw* set and on the set of the spinoff show called *Hee Haw Honeys.* He played my husband on the *Honeys,* so I was blessed to be around even more of his laughter than the others.

In one scene he was in the judge's spot, and before he knew what was happening, his pants slipped down to the floor. He just stood there and dared anyone to laugh. Of course, all of us were laughing so hard we couldn't stop. He finally just gave in to the laughter, and we all had to stop long enough to catch a breath before we could move on. He was such a good-natured man, it just made everything easier.

I had many occasions to talk of life and meaningful things with this wonderful man. It was precious to know about his relationship with the Lord, which truly meant something in his life. He worked hard to send his son to seminary where he learned to serve the Lord well with music, and his daughter to college, where she would meet and marry a minister.

Many people have asked if Kenny knew the Lord. I know he did in a real way. His sons and daughter are lovely children and a precious reflection of their parents. Kenny and Donna were wonderful friends, and I admired their love for all. I will always remember how Kenny looked at life through the eyes of laughter and music, driven by love.

We were preparing to do an album of duets of the old songs of faith when Kenny went on to be with the Lord. His legacy is one of the things that even today make my heart beat with a passion, and for that I salute my precious friend! Sa-loote! We'll do that duet in heaven, my precious friend. Yes, we will!

Kenny Price

What can I get you?

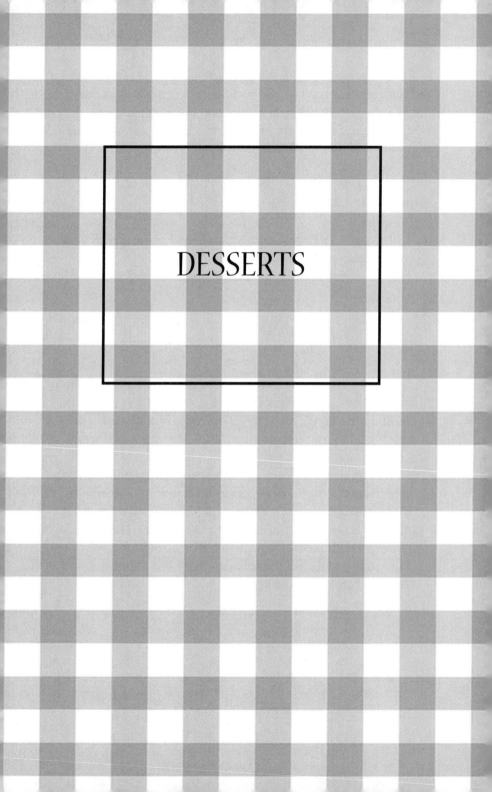

DESSERTS

I just love sweets and all things made of fruit. Lots of these recipes combine my two loves. Others are just wonderful things I've discovered over the years. Just dive into these with gusto and forget about counting calories and other such nonsense. Dessert was created to be enjoyed, so ENJOY!

Heath Bar Cheesecake

1   *18-ounce package refrigerated oatmeal cookie dough with chocolate and butterscotch chips*
2   *8-ounce packages cream cheese, softened*
2   *eggs*
½   *cup sugar*
1   *teaspoon vanilla extract*
4   *1.4-ounce Heath candy bars, coarsely chopped*

Preheat the oven to 350°. Coat a 9-inch deep-dish pie plate with nonstick cooking spray. Slice the cookie dough into 24 slices and arrange them on the bottom and up the sides of the pie plate. Press the dough together, making a uniform crust, and set aside.

In a large bowl, with an electric beater on medium speed, beat the cream cheese, eggs, sugar, and vanilla for 1 minute, until well mixed. Stir in the candy pieces and pour the mixture into the pie plate. Bake for 40 to 45 minutes, until the center is firm. Remove from the oven and allow to cool. Cover loosely and chill for at least 4 hours or overnight.

Makes 8 to 10 servings.

Carrot Fruit Jumbles

2½	cups all-purpose flour
1	teaspoon baking soda
½	teaspoon baking powder
½	teaspoon ground cloves
2	teaspoon cinnamon
¼	teaspoon salt
1	cup quick cooking oats
¾	cup packed brown sugar
¼	cup sugar
1	cup salted butter, softened
2	large eggs
2	teaspoons pure vanilla extract
2	cups grated carrots
½	cup crushed pineapple, drained
1	cup chopped walnuts

Preheat the oven to 350 degree F. In a medium bowl, combine the flour, baking soda, baking powder, cloves, cinnamon, salt, and oats. Mix them well and set aside.

In the bowl of an electric mixer, blend the sugars; add the butter and mix to form a grainy paste. Add the eggs and vanilla, beating at medium speed until light and fluffy. Add the carrots, pineapple, and nuts and blend until combined. The batter will be lumpy. Add the flour mixture and blend at low speed until just combined. Do not over mix. Drop by rounded teaspoons onto an ungreased baking sheet. Bake for 13 to 15 minutes. Immediately transfer the cookies to wire racks to cool.

Makes 4 dozen cookies.

Crazy Good Cranberry Nut Bread

2	cups all-purpose flour
¾	cup white sugar
¾	teaspoon salt
1½	teaspoons baking powder
½	teaspoon baking soda
1	cup coarsely chopped cranberries
½	cup chopped nuts
1	egg
2	tablespoons vegetable oil
¾	cup orange juice
1	tablespoon grated orange peel

Preheat the oven to 350°. Grease a 9x5-inch loaf pan. In a mixing bowl, combine the flour, sugar, salt, baking powder, and baking soda. Add the cranberries and chopped nuts and stir to coat them with the flour mixture.

In a small bowl, combine the egg, oil, orange juice, and grated orange peel; add to the flour mixture and stir until it is just combined. Spoon the batter into the prepared pan and bake for 50 minutes or until a toothpick comes out clean.

Let the bread sit for 10 minutes, then remove from the pan and place on a cooling rack. Let the loaf cool completely before slicing.

Makes 1 loaf of bread.

I love, love, love, shortbread!! Here are a few of my favorites.

Lulu's Lip Smackin' Shortbread

2	cups all-purpose flour
½	cup confectioners' sugar
¼	teaspoon salt
¼	teaspoon baking powder
1	teaspoon vanilla extract
1	cup butter or margarine, softened
2	tablespoons granulated sugar

Preheat the oven to 350°. In a large bowl, beat the flour, confectioners' sugar, salt, baking powder, vanilla, and butter at medium speed until it is well mixed. Pat the dough into a 9-inch round pan and prick it well with a fork. Sprinkle the granulated sugar over the dough. Bake for 30 to 35 minutes. Cut into wedges while warm, and cool on a wire rack. Separate the cookies.
Makes 6 to 8 cookies.

Linda Thompson and LuLu

Jumpin' Java Shortbread Cookies

½   cup almonds, finely ground
1¼   cups sifted all-purpose flour
¾   cup confectioners' sugar
2   tablespoons instant coffee
¾   cup butter or margarine, softened
     Granulated sugar

In a large bowl, combine the almonds, flour, confectioners' sugar, and coffee. Blend in the butter and mix until well blended. Shape the dough into a ball and wrap it in foil or plastic. Refrigerate the dough for at least 30 minutes.

On a lightly floured surface roll the chilled dough to about a ¼-inch thickness. Cut with a 2-inch cookie cutter. Place the cookies 1 inch apart on an ungreased cookie sheet and sprinkle the tops with granulated sugar. Bake for 10 to 12 minutes or until the edges are just firm. Remove the cookies from the sheet and cool them on a wire rack

Makes about 2 dozen cookies.

Shortbread Supreme

2   cups sifted all-purpose flour
1   cup butter or margarine
½   cup sugar
½   teaspoon vanilla extract

Preheat the oven to 350°. In a medium mixing bowl, cream the butter, vanilla, and sugar until fluffy. Add the flour and knead the dough until it breaks smoothly. If extra flour is required, add in small quantities.

Roll the dough to a ¼-inch thickness and cut into patterns (hearts, diamonds, rabbits, and so forth). Bake the cookies for 12 to 15 minutes until lightly golden brown on top.

Makes about 2 dozen cookies.

Almond Shortbread

1	cup butter
½	cup white sugar
2	teaspoons almond extract
2½	cups sifted all-purpose flour
	White sugar

In a large bowl, beat the butter, sugar, and almond extract until light and fluffy. With a wooden spoon, stir the mixture until it is smooth and well combined. Divide the dough into 2 parts. Refrigerate, covered, for 2 hours.

Preheat the oven to 300°. On a lightly sugared surface, roll out the dough, one part at a time, about ½-inch thick. Using a 1½-inch round cookie cutter, cut out cookies and place them 1 inch apart on an ungreased cookie sheet. With the end of a wooden spoon or a cookie press, make an indentation in the center of each cookie.

Bake for 25 to 30 minutes or until light golden brown around the edges. While the cookies are still warm, roll them in sugar. Cool completely on wire rack.

Makes about 3 dozen cookies.

With Kris Kristofferson and Rita Coolidge

Lemon Shortbread Cookies

½	*cup butter or margarine, softened*
¼	*cup packed brown sugar*
2	*teaspoons grated lemon zest*
½	*teaspoon lemon extract*
¼	*teaspoon vanilla extract*
1	*cup all-purpose flour*
¼	*teaspoon salt*

Preheat the oven to 325°. In a medium bowl, beat the butter or margarine and brown sugar with an electric mixer on medium speed until it is light and fluffy. Beat in the lemon zest, lemon extract, and vanilla extract. Add the flour and salt to the butter/sugar mixture and blend well. Turn the dough onto a lightly floured surface, and roll out to ¼-inch thickness. Cut out cookies using a 2-inch round cutter and place 2 inches apart on ungreased cookie sheets. Reroll the scraps and repeat the process until all the dough is used.

Bake for 20 to 25 minutes until the cookies are a pale, golden nut brown. Let them stand for 2 minutes, remove them to a rack, and let them cool completely.

Makes about 2 dozen cookies.

On the Hee Haw *set*

Molly's Classic Chocolate and Coffee Pound Cake

My dear friend Molly (Camille) makes this and oh, my gosh, it is spectacular!

3	cups all-purpose flour
1½	teaspoons baking powder
½	teaspoon salt
4	ounces unsweetened chocolate
¼	cup strong brewed coffee
1	cup butter, softened
1	cup sugar
5	eggs
⅔	cup whipping cream
2	teaspoons vanilla extract
2	tablespoons brandy
	Whipped cream

In a large bowl, combine the flour, baking powder, and salt. Sift them again and set aside. In the top of a double boiler over simmering water, heat the chocolate and coffee, stirring constantly until the mixture is smooth and satiny. Set it aside to cool.

Preheat the oven to 300°. In the large bowl of an electric mixer, combine the butter and sugar. Add the eggs and beat hard until the mixture is smooth. Add the flour mixture alternately with the chocolate/coffee mixture and whipping cream. Blend in the vanilla and brandy.

Spoon the batter into a well-greased and floured 10-inch tube or bundt pan. Bake for 1½ to 1¾ hours. Cool the cake before slicing. Serve with whipped cream or your favorite sauce.

Makes 12 servings.

Easy Chocolate Mousse Pie

Crust:
⅓   *cup melted butter*
1¼   *cup chocolate wafer crumbs*
¼   *cup sugar*

Filling:
½   *pint heavy cream*
5½   *ounces Hershey's chocolate syrup*
1   *tablespoon confectioners' sugar*
       Chocolate wafer crumbs for topping

In a medium saucepan, melt the butter and stir in the crumbs and sugar. Press the mixture against the sides and bottom of a 9-inch pie pan. Bake at 450° oven for 5 minutes. Chill.

In a small mixing bowl, whip the cream and add the syrup just before the cream stiffens. Mix in the sugar. Pour the filling into the crust and sprinkle with the remaining chocolate wafer crumbs, then freeze. Remove from the freezer 10 minutes before serving. Add extra whipped cream on top of the pie and fresh fruit or chocolate curls as garnish.
Makes 6 to 8 servings.

Chocolate Bread Pudding with Dried Cranberries

¼   *cup (½ stick) unsalted butter, melted*
1   *cup sugar*
4   *large eggs*
1   *cup milk*
1   *cup unsweetened cocoa powder*
1   *tablespoon vanilla extract*
1   *24-inch loaf French bread, cubed*
2   *cups dried cranberries*

Preheat the oven to 350°. In a large bowl, beat together the butter, sugar, and eggs. Add the milk and mix, then stir in the cocoa and then the vanilla. Toss in the bread cubes and cranberries, mixing well.

Butter a baking dish and pour the egg mixture into it. Place the baking dish in a larger ovenproof pan and pour hot water into it until the water is about 1 inch deep. Bake for 45 minutes or until set. Serve with cinnamon flavored whipped cream.

Makes 6 servings.

Biscottini (Little Dippin' Cookies)

1	*cup (2 sticks) butter*
1½	*cups sugar*
3	*eggs*
2	*teaspoons vanilla, anise, or almond extract*
5	*cups all-purpose flour (approximately)*
2	*teaspoons baking powder*
½	*cup chopped nuts*

In a large mixing bowl, cream the butter and sugar. Add the eggs and the vanilla flavoring. Sift the flour and baking powder together and add the nuts. Add the flour mixture gradually to the egg mixture by hand; the batter should be firm. You may need to add more flour or a few teaspoons of milk to get the dough to the right texture.

Shape the dough into loaves about 3 inches wide and place them on greased cookie sheets or a jellyroll pan. Bake at 350° for about 20 minutes or until very light brown. Remove from the oven. Cool and slice into ½-inch slices. Place the slices on the cookie sheets and bake them at 375° for about 10 minutes, then turn them and toast the other side.

Makes about 4 dozen cookies.

Nothin' To It Black Forest Torte

1   *18.25-ounce box chocolate cake mix*
2   *cups whipped cream*
       Sugar to taste
1   *17-ounce can sour cherries*
       Chocolate slivers
       Maraschino cherries

Prepare and bake the cake mix according to the directions on the package. Allow it to cool completely.

In a mixing bowl, sweeten the whipped cream with the sugar as needed. Fold in the drained sour cherries, and spread the mixture over the cake mix. Top everything with the chocolate slivers and maraschino cherries.

Makes 8 to 10 servings.

Snowballs

These are great to make with kids!

1   *6-ounce package semisweet chocolate pieces*
⅓   *cup evaporated milk*
1   *cup confectioners' sugar, sifted*
½   *cup chopped pecans*
1   *3½-ounce can flaked coconut*

In the top of a double boiler over simmering water, combine the chocolate and milk and heat until the chocolate melts. Stir the mixture until blended. Remove it from the heat and stir in the confectioners' sugar and pecans. Cool slightly and form the mixture into 1-inch balls and roll in the coconut.

Makes 24 snowballs.

Cranberry Noel Cookies
A Christmas Favorite of Damon's

1	cup (2 sticks) butter, softened
½	cup sugar
2	tablespoons milk
1	teaspoon vanilla extract
½	teaspoon salt
2½	cups flour, sifted
¾	cup finely chopped dried cranberries
½	cup pecans, toasted
1½	cups shredded coconut

In a mixing bowl, beat the butter and sugar until they are light and fluffy. Add the milk, vanilla, and salt. Gradually add the flour and stir in the cranberries and pecans. Divide the dough into 2 balls and form each ball into a log. Roll the logs in the coconut. Chill for several hours. Slice and bake at 375° for 10 to 12 minutes. The cookies will not spread or turn brown.
Makes about 3 dozen cookies.

LuLu and Damon

Holiday Cookies

I make them all year long.

1	cup butter
2	cups light brown sugar
2	eggs
1	teaspoon vanilla extract
½	cup buttermilk
3½	cups all-purpose flour
1	teaspoon baking soda
1	teaspoon salt
1½	cups chopped pecans
1	cup sweetened flaked coconut
2	cups halved candied cherries
1	cup chopped dates

In the large bowl of an electric mixer, combine the butter, brown sugar, eggs, and vanilla thoroughly, then stir in the buttermilk. In a separate bowl, sift the flour, baking soda, and salt together, then add them to the wet mixture. Stir in the nuts, coconut, cherries, and dates. Chill for at least 1 hour.

Preheat the oven to 400°. Drop the batter by teaspoonfuls 2 inches apart onto a lightly greased baking sheet. Bake for 8 to 10 minutes.

Makes 24 cookies.

Ultimate Chocolate Peanut Butter Cake

12	ounces semi sweet chocolate bits
½	pound unsalted butter
½	cup peanut butter
⅓	cup sugar
½	cup cognac, bourbon, or water

2   tablespoons cornstarch
6   eggs

Icing:
1   cup whipping cream
1   tablespoon butter
12   ounces semisweet chocolate bits

Butter a 10-inch springform pan. Preheat the oven to 350°. In a heavy saucepan, combine the chocolate bits, butter, peanut butter, and sugar. Place over low heat, stirring occasionally, until the chocolate and butter are melted. Remove the mixture from the heat and cool it slightly. In a small bowl combine the cognac and cornstarch and stir until smooth. In a large bowl whisk the eggs briefly.

Add the cornstarch mixture to the eggs and beat to combine them. Add about a fourth of the warm chocolate mixture, beating it vigorously to prevent the eggs from cooking. Add the remaining chocolate mixture and beat it until it is smooth and slightly thickened, about 50 strokes. Pour the batter into the springform pan. Bake at 350° for 20 to 30 minutes, just until set. Remove the cake from the oven and cool it completely.

For the icing, heat the cream almost to a boil in the microwave. Place the butter and chocolate in a medium bowl and pour the hot cream over the chocolate and butter. Let the mixture stand for 5 minutes, then beat it with a spoon until it is smooth.

Run the knife around the edge of the pan to loosen the cake and remove the sides of the pan. Place the cake on a wire rack and place the rack in a large shallow pan. Pour the icing over the cake, allowing it to drip down the sides to completely cover the top and sides of the cake. Let it stand until the icing is firm, and chill in the refrigerator. Remove from the refrigerator 30 minutes before serving. This is a rich dessert.

Makes 10 servings when cut into thin slices.

Heavenly Harvest Carrot Cake

2 cups all-purpose flour
2 teaspoons baking soda
2 teaspoons cinnamon
½ teaspoon salt
3 eggs
¾ cup vegetable oil
¾ cup buttermilk
2 cups sugar
2 teaspoons vanilla extract
1 8-ounce can crushed pineapple, drained
2 cups grated carrots
3½ ounces shredded coconut
1 cup chopped walnuts

Buttermilk Glaze:
1 cup sugar
½ teaspoon baking soda
½ cup buttermilk
¼ pound butter or margarine
¼ cup corn syrup
1 teaspoon vanilla extract

Cream Cheese Frosting:
¼ pound butter or margarine at room temperature
1 8-ounce package cream cheese, at room temperature
1 teaspoon vanilla extract
2 cups confectioners' sugar
1 teaspoon orange juice
1 teaspoon grated orange rind

Preheat the oven to 350°. Generously grease a 9x13-inch baking dish or two 9-inch cake pans and set aside. Sift together the flour, baking soda, cinnamon, and salt and set it aside. In a large bowl, beat the eggs. Add the oil, buttermilk, sugar, and vanilla, and mix well. Add the flour mixture, pineapple, carrots, coconut, and walnuts and stir well. Pour the batter into the prepared baking dish and bake for 50 to 55 minutes or until a wood toothpick inserted in the center comes out clean.

For the glaze: In a small saucepan, combine the sugar, baking soda, buttermilk, butter or margarine, and corn syrup and bring it to a boil. Cook for 5 minutes, stirring occasionally. Remove from the heat and stir in the vanilla. Slowly pour the glaze over the hot cake. Cool the cake in the pan until the glaze is totally absorbed, about 15 minutes. Turn out of the pan if desired. Cool it completely.

For the frosting: Beat together the butter or margarine and cream cheese until it is fluffy. Add the vanilla, confectioners' sugar, orange juice, and orange peel and mix until it is smooth. Once the cake is thoroughly cooled, spread the frosting on the cake. Refrigerate the cake until the frosting is set. The cake may be refrigerated for several days.

Makes 20 to 24 servings.

A game of cards

Dipped Chocolate Chip Cookies
The more chocolate the better, honey!

2¼	*cups all-purpose flour*
1	*teaspoon baking soda*
1	*teaspoon salt*
1	*cup butter, softened*
¾	*cup sugar*
¾	*cup firmly packed brown sugar*
1	*teaspoon vanilla extract*
2	*eggs*
12	*ounces semisweet chocolate chips*

Chocolate Dip:

1	*6-ounce bag semisweet chocolate morsels*
1	*6-ounce bag white chocolate morsels*
	Vegetable oil

Preheat the oven to 375°. In a small bowl, combine the flour, baking soda, and salt and set the mixture aside. In a large bowl, combine the butter, sugars, and vanilla extract and mix until it is creamy. Beat in the eggs and gradually add the flour mixture. Stir in the chocolate chips. Drop by level teaspoons onto ungreased baking sheets and bake for 9 to 11 minutes. The cookies should still be soft when removed from the oven. Place them on cooling racks.

In separate small saucepans, melt the semisweet and white chocolate morsels and add a small amount of the vegetable oil in each saucepan. Dip each cookie halfway into the dark chocolate and return to the rack to cool. After it is cooled, dip the other half into the white chocolate and allow them to cool.

Makes about 3 dozen cookies.

Old-Fashioned Southern Bread Pudding
This pudding won't make it past midnight, guaranteed!

1¼	cups sugar, divided
½	teaspoon cinnamon
8	cups day-old egg bread cut into ½-inch cubes
¼	cup butter, melted
⅓	raisins
1	quart half and half
8	large eggs, lightly beaten
1	tablespoon vanilla extract

Preheat the oven to 400°. Grease a 9x13-inch baking dish. In a medium bowl, combine ¼ cup of the sugar with the cinnamon. In a large bowl, toss the bread cubes, melted butter, and raisins, and the sugar-cinnamon mixture. Spread the dough evenly in a greased pan and set it aside.

In a small bowl, whisk the eggs lightly. In a small saucepan, bring the cream, remaining sugar, and vanilla to a boil. Gradually whisk the cream mixture into the eggs and pour over the bread mixture. Place the pan in a water bath and bake for 35 to 40 minutes until the custard sets and the top is golden brown.
Makes 8 servings.

My favorite candy recipes have kept my friends begging for more every year. I usually make these during the holidays and send them to loved ones.

Berry Nutty Candy

1   *pound white chocolate*
1   *14-ounce can sweetened condensed milk*
     Pecans
     Candied cherries or blueberries

In a small saucepan, melt the white chocolate and stir in the sweetened condensed milk. Stir in the pecans and cherries. Pour the mixture into a square baking dish and refrigerate until it is set. Cut into small squares.
   Makes 24 to 30 candies.

Coconut Candy

1   *14-ounce bag coconut*
2   *16-ounce boxes confectioners' sugar*
1   *14-ounce can sweetened condensed milk*
½   *cup (1 stick) butter*
¼   *cup chopped pecans*
     Melted chocolate

In a mixing bowl, combine the coconut, confectioners' sugar, milk, butter, and pecans and shape the mixture into squares. Dip the squares into the melted chocolate and let them cool on waxed paper.
   Makes 48 candies.

Peanut Butter Balls

1½   *cups peanut butter*
½   *cup lightly salted butter*
1   *teaspoon vanilla extract*
1   *16-ounce box confectioners' sugar*
     Melted chocolate

In a mixing bowl, combine the peanut butter, butter, vanilla, and confectioners' sugar. Roll the mixture into balls and dip them into the melted chocolate. Let the balls cool on a sheet of waxed paper.
Makes 20 to 24 balls.

Pralines

Justin's weakness!

2   *cups sugar*
1   *cup buttermilk*
1   *tablespoon baking soda*
1   *pinch salt*
1   *teaspoon vanilla extract*
2   *tablespoons butter*
1   *pound pecans*

In a mixing bowl, combine the sugar, buttermilk, baking soda, and salt and cook to the soft-ball state. Mix in the pecans, vanilla, and butter until the batter loses its gloss. Butter 2 spoons and spoon the pralines onto a buttered sheet of waxed paper.
Makes 36 to 40 pralines.

Orange Balls

These deserve a fancier name because they taste so decadent.

1	6-ounce can orange juice, undiluted
½	cup (1 stick) butter, room temperature
1	16-ounce box confectioners' sugar
1	3½-ounce can coconut
1	cup chopped nuts
1	7¼-ounce box vanilla wafers

Mix together all ingredients in a medium bowl. Roll the mixture into balls and roll them in the confectioners' sugar to coat.
   Makes 36 balls.

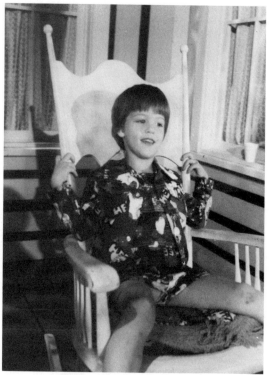

Damon on the Hee Haw *set*

Georgia Peach Custard

1	tablespoon unsalted butter
½	cup plus 1 tablespoonful sugar
3	cups peeled, sliced peaches
3	large eggs, beaten
2	teaspoons pure vanilla extract
6	tablespoons all-purpose flour
1½	cups heavy cream
1	tablespoon cinnamon

Preheat the oven to 375°. Lightly grease a 10-inch round baking dish with butter and sprinkle with 1 tablespoon of the sugar. Arrange the peaches on the bottom of the dish.

In a medium-sized bowl, beat the eggs until fluffy. Add the vanilla, flour, cream, and cinnamon and whisk them together well. Let the mixture rest for a few minutes. Pour the batter over the peaches and bake it for about 40 minutes, until the custard is firm. Serve warm or at room temperature.
Makes 8 servings.

With Burt Convey
on the Love Boat *set*

Simple Chocolate Sheet Cake

This is the cake that got my Justin in a heap of trouble and left me rolling on the floor with laughter!

1	tablespoon butter
¾	cup cocoa, preferably Dutch processed
1¼	cups all-purpose flour
¼	teaspoon salt
8	ounces semisweet chocolate, chopped
12	tablespoons unsalted butter, plus extra for greasing the pan
4	large eggs
1½	cups sugar
1	teaspoon vanilla extract
1	cup buttermilk
½	teaspoon baking soda

Adjust the oven rack to the middle position and preheat the oven to 325°. Coat the bottom and sides of a 9x13-inch pan with 1 tablespoon of butter. In a medium bowl, sift together the cocoa, flour, and salt and set the mixture aside. In a microwave-safe bowl covered with plastic wrap, heat the chocolate and butter for 2 minutes at 50% power, and stir until smooth.

In a medium bowl, whisk together the eggs, sugar, and vanilla. Whisk the chocolate into the egg mixture until combined. In a mixing bowl, combine the buttermilk and baking soda and whisk into the chocolate mixture. Then whisk in the dry ingredients until the batter is just blended. Pour the batter into the prepared pan and bake until it is firm in the center when lightly pressed and a wooden toothpick comes out clean, about 40 minutes. Cool the cake on a wire rack until it reaches room temperature, at least 1 hour. Serve as is or ice with Creamy Milk Chocolate Frosting (recipe follows).
Makes 8 to 12 servings.

Creamy Milk Chocolate Frosting

½   *cup heavy cream*
       Pinch salt
1   *tablespoon light or dark corn syrup*
10   *ounces milk chocolate*
½   *cup confectioners' sugar*
8   *tablespoons cold unsalted butter, cut into 8 pieces*

In a microwave-safe measuring cup, heat the cream, salt, and corn syrup in microwave-safe measuring cup on high until the mixture simmers, about 1 minute, or bring it to simmer in a small saucepan over medium heat. Place the chocolate in the work bowl of a food processor fitted with a steel blade. With the machine running, gradually add the hot cream mixture through the feed tube. Process for 1 minute after the cream has been added. Stop the machine and add the confectioners' sugar to the bowl and process the mixture to combine the ingredients, about 30 seconds. With the machine running, add the butter through the feed tube 1 tablespoon at a time; process the mixture until the butter is incorporated and the mixture is smooth, about 20 seconds longer. Transfer the frosting to a medium bowl and cool at room temperature, stirring frequently, until it is thick and spreadable, about 1 hour.

Makes frosting for 1 sheet cake.

Make Ahead Carrot Cake

4	cups all-purpose flour
4	teaspoons baking soda
4	teaspoons cinnamon
1	teaspoon salt
6	eggs
1½	cups vegetable oil
1½	cups buttermilk
4	cups sugar
4	teaspoons vanilla extract
8	ounces crushed pineapple, drained
4	cups grated carrots
6	ounces shredded coconut
2	cups walnut pieces
	Buttermilk Glaze (recipe follows)
	Cream Cheese Frosting (recipe follows)

Preheat the oven to 350°. Generously grease a 10x15-inch cake pan. In a mixing bowl, sift the flour, baking soda, cinnamon, and salt together and set aside.

In a separate bowl, beat the eggs, then add the oil, buttermilk, sugar, and vanilla to egg mixture and mix well. Add the sifted flour mixture, pineapple, carrots, coconut, and walnuts to the egg mixture and mix well. Pour the batter into the prepared cake pan and bake for 45 minutes or until a wooden toothpick inserted in the center of the cake comes out clean.

Remove the cake from the oven. Using a dinner fork, punch 10 to 12 holes in the top of the cake and slowly pour the buttermilk glaze over the hot cake. Cool the cake in a pan until the glaze is totally absorbed, about 15 minutes. Place it in a refrigerator and cool completely.

Prepare the cream cheese frosting and frost the cake when it is completely cool. Refrigerate until the frosting sets. Wrap in plastic wrap, using caution not to damage the frosting. Can be kept refrigerated for up to 3 days before serving.

Makes 1 cake.

Buttermilk Glaze:

⅓   pound (about 1⅓ cups) sugar
½   teaspoon baking soda
⅓   cup buttermilk
½   cup (1 stick) butter
1   tablespoon corn syrup
1   teaspoon vanilla extract

In a saucepan, combine the sugar, baking soda, buttermilk, butter, and corn syrup. Bring the mixture to a boil and cook for 5 minutes, stirring occasionally. Remove it from the heat and stir in the vanilla. Use immediately on the warm carrot cake.

Cream Cheese Frosting:

⅓   pound butter, at room temperature
1   pound cream cheese
2   tablespoons vanilla extract
1⅓ pounds confectioners' sugar
     Juice and grated peel of ½ orange

In a mixing bowl, cream the butter and cream cheese together with an electric mixer until the mixture is fluffy. Using a spatula, scrape down the sides of the bowl. Add the vanilla, confectioners' sugar, orange juice, and orange peel and mix on slow speed until the frosting is smooth.

No-Bake Fudge Cookies

These are great in the summer when it's too hot to turn on the oven.

2	*cups sugar*
½	*cup milk*
¼	*teaspoon salt*
⅓	*cup cocoa*
½	*cup (1 stick) margarine*
1	*teaspoon vanilla extract*
½	*cup peanut butter*
3	*cups Quaker Instant Oats*

In a large saucepan, mix together the sugar, milk, salt, cocoa, margarine, and vanilla over medium heat. Bring the mixture to a boil and cook for 1 to 3 minutes. Remove the mixture from the heat and stir in the peanut butter and oats. Drop the batter by teaspoonfuls onto waxed paper and allow them to cool.

Makes about 4 dozen cookies.

High School Graduation—I'm the blond right of center

Granny Smith Apple Fritters

1	cup all-purpose flour
1½	teaspoon baking powder
½	teaspoon salt
1	egg
½	cup apple cider
1	tablespoon melted margarine
1	tablespoon sugar
1½	cups peeled and finely chopped Granny Smith apples
¼	teaspoon cinnamon
¼	teaspoon vanilla extract
	Peanut oil for frying
	Confectioners' sugar

In a mixing bowl, combine the flour, baking powder, and salt. In another bowl, combine the egg, cider, margarine, sugar, apples, cinnamon, and vanilla and add to the dry mixture, stirring until incorporated. Do not over mix.

Preheat the peanut oil in a skillet to 350°. Drop the balls of apple mixture from a tablespoon into the hot oil and fry to golden brown (about 2 minutes on each side). Drain the balls on a paper towel and roll them in confectioners' sugar.

Makes 24 small or 12 large fritters.

Yummy Strawberry Tarts

½   cup butter or margarine
¾   cup plus 1 tablespoon sugar, divided
2   eggs, divided
1   tablespoon milk
½   cup all-purpose flour
¼   teaspoon baking powder
6   ounces all-fruit strawberry spread
1½   cups flaked coconut

Preheat the oven to 400°. Grease the top of two 2- to 2½-inch muffin pans of 12 muffin cups each and set them aside. In a medium bowl, beat together the butter and ¼ cup of sugar until the mixture is light and fluffy. Add one egg and the milk. In a small bowl combine the flour and baking powder. Add the flour mixture to the liquid mixture. Beat into a soft dough.

On a lightly floured surface, roll the dough to ⅛-inch thickness. With a 3-inch scalloped round biscuit cutter, cut the dough into 24 rounds. Place the rounds over the top of each muffin cup and press to indent slightly. Place a spoonful of strawberry spread in each indent.

In a small bowl, place the remaining tablespoon of sugar, 1 egg, and coconut. Mix until they are well blended and place a spoonful of the coconut mixture on each tart. Bake for 10 to 15 minutes until golden.

Makes 24 tarts.

Kahlua Chocolate Mousse

4	ounces unsweetened chocolate
1/4	cup (2 ounces) unsalted butter
2	ounces Kahlua liqueur*
4	large eggs, separated
1	cup sugar divided
2	cups heavy cream

(You can use 2 ounces of chocolate syrup and 1/2 teaspoon of instant coffee to replace the Kahlua if desired.)

In the top of a double boiler over simmering water melt the chocolate and butter. Whisk 1/2 cup of sugar with the egg yolks until light and lemon colored (2 to 4 minutes), then whisk in the Kahlua. In a small bowl, temper some of the warm chocolate into the egg yolks. In a large bowl, whisk the heavy cream with 1/4 cup of sugar until it is fairly stiff.

In a small bowl, whisk the egg whites with 1/4 of sugar until soft peaks form. Carefully mix the Kahlua base into the whipped cream until it is smooth and one color. Whip some of the egg whites into the Kahlua base, then fold in the rest so it doesn't deflate. Place in a refrigerator for at least 10 minutes before serving.

Makes 4 to 6 servings.

Norman's Pecan Fudge Pie

½   cup (1 stick) butter
4   1-ounce squares unsweetened chocolate
4   eggs, lightly beaten
3   tablespoon light corn syrup
1½   cups sugar
¼   teaspoon salt
1   teaspoon vanilla extract
1   cup chopped pecans
1   9-inch pie shell

In the top of a double boiler or in a saucepan over low heat, melt the butter and chocolate. In a medium bowl, combine the beaten eggs, corn syrup, sugar, salt, vanilla, and pecans and mix well. Add the chocolate mixture and mix thoroughly. Pour the filling into the pie shell. Bake in a 350° oven for 30 to 35 minutes until the filling is set, but soft inside.
  Makes 6 to 8 servings.

With Junior Samples

Carrot Spice Cake

1¼   cups sugar
¾   cup light corn syrup
¾   cup skim milk
8   egg whites
2   cups self-rising flour
2   teaspoons ground cinnamon
2   cups shredded carrots

In a large mixing bowl, beat the sugar, corn syrup, milk, and egg whites. In a bowl, combine the flour and cinnamon and add them to the batter. Beat the mixture well. Stir the carrots into the batter and pour it into a greased and floured 10-inch fluted tube pan. Bake at 350° for 1 hour, then cool in the pan for 10 minutes. Invert the cake onto a wire rack and cool completely.
Makes 16 servings.

Pineapple Fluff Cake
I bring this out at the end of my summer barbecues and enjoy it while we watch the sun go down!

1   4.6-ounce box instant vanilla pudding
1   14-ounce can crushed pineapple
1   8-ounce carton Cool Whip
     Prepared angel food, pound, or yellow cake
     Cherries

In a mixing bowl, combine the dried pudding with the crushed pineapple (do not drain). Fold in the Cool Whip. Slice the cake lengthwise, spread each layer with the cream mixture, and garnish with the cherries.
Makes 6 to 8 servings.

Strawberry-Filled French Toast

This makes Saturday mornings special when my boys come to visit their Momma.

½	*cup chopped strawberries*
½	*cup strawberry-flavored cream cheese*
8	*slices white or wheat bread*
2	*eggs, beaten*
¼	*cup milk*
1	*tablespoon butter*
	Strawberries
	Syrup

In a mixing bowl, stir together the chopped strawberries and cream cheese until they are well blended. Spread equal amounts of the cheese mixture on 4 slices of the bread and top them with the remaining 4 slices of bread.

In a shallow bowl, combine the eggs and milk. Melt the butter in a large skillet over medium heat. Dip both sides of each sandwich into the egg mixture and cook in the skillet, turning once until both sides are golden brown. Garnish with strawberries and serve with syrup.

Makes 4 servings of French toast.

Misty Rowe, Gunella Hutton, and LuLu

Strawberry Heart Cake
You can't have Valentine's Day without this creation!

1	18¼-ounce box Sweet Rewards reduced fat white cake mix
⅓	cup canola oil
2	large eggs
2	large egg whites
1	3-ounce package strawberry gelatin
½	10-ounce package frozen sliced strawberries
½	cup skim milk

Strawberry Frosting:
3	tablespoons margarine
1	16-ounce box confectioners' sugar
½	10-ounce package frozen sliced strawberries

Preheat the oven to 350°. Spray 1 9-inch square pan and 1 9-inch round pan with baking spray and dust with flour. In a mixing bowl, combine the cake mix, oil, eggs, egg whites, strawberry gelatin, ½ cup strawberries, and skim milk, mixing well until they are well blended. Divide the batter and pour into the prepared pans. Bake for 20 to 25 minutes or until a wooden toothpick inserted in the center of one of the cakes comes out clean. Remove from the pans and cool completely.

To form a heart, cut the round cake in half and place each half with the cut side next to the square side. You may need to trim down the corners to get a heart-shaped cake. Turn the cake so the end of the square cake is pointed downward and the round halves are at the top, making a heart shaped cake.

To make the frosting, mix together the margarine, confectioner's sugar, and strawberries until they are well blended. Spread on the top and sides of the cake.

Makes 16 servings.

Classic Crème Brûlée

8	egg yolks
⅓	cup sugar
2	cups heavy cream
1	teaspoon pure vanilla extract
6	Custard cups
¼	cup sugar (for caramelized tops)

Preheat the oven to 300°. In a large bowl, whisk together the egg yolks and sugar until the sugar has dissolved and the mixture is thick and pale yellow. Add the cream and vanilla and continue to whisk until it is well blended. Strain the mixture into a large bowl, skimming off any foam or bubbles. Divide the mixture among 6 ramekins or custard cups. Place them in a water bath and bake until the mixture is set around the edges, but still loose in the center, about 40 to 50 minutes.

Remove the custards from the oven and leave them in the water bath until cooled. Remove the cups from the water and chill for at least 2 hours (up to 2 days).

When ready to serve, sprinkle about 2 teaspoons of sugar over each custard. For the best results, use a small, hand-held torch to melt the sugar. If you don't have a torch, place them under the broiler until the sugar melts. Rechill the custards for a few minutes before serving.

Makes 6 servings.

Refreshing Gelatin Salad

1	3-ounce package lime gelatin
1	3-ounce package lemon gelatin
1	cup hot water
1½	cups cold water
1	12-ounce can crushed pineapple
3	bananas, chopped
½	16-ounce package miniature marshmallows
½	cup sugar
1	tablespoon cornstarch
1	egg, beaten
½	cup whipping cream
	Sugar to taste
	Juice of ½ lemon
½	teaspoon vanilla extract
1	cup shredded sharp Cheddar cheese

In a medium size bowl, dissolve the lime and lemon gelatin in the hot water. Stir in the cold water. Drain the pineapple, reserving 1 cup of the juice. Add the pineapple, bananas, and marshmallows to the gelatin mixture, stirring well. Pour into a 9x13-inch dish and chill until firm.

In a medium saucepan, combine the sugar, cornstarch, egg, and reserved pineapple juice and bring to a boil. Cook until the mixture thickens, stirring constantly. Chill thoroughly.

In the bowl of an electric mixer, beat the whipping cream until soft peaks form. Add the sugar, lemon juice, and vanilla, beating until stiff peaks form. Fold into the chilled pineapple juice mixture. Spread over the congealed gelatin mixture. Top with the Cheddar cheese.

Makes 10 to 12 servings.

Granny's Fudge Cake

4   ounces unsweetened chocolate
2   cups sugar
1   cup butter
4   eggs
2   cups minus 2 tablespoons flour
1   cup chopped pecans
2   teaspoon vanilla extract

Fudge Frosting:
2   cups sugar
⅔   cup milk
¼   teaspoon salt
2   ounces unsweetened baking chocolate
½   cup shortening or butter
2   teaspoons vanilla extract

In the top of a double boiler, melt the chocolate over hot water, stirring frequently. Remove from the heat and set aside.

In the bowl of an electric mixer, cream the sugar and butter until they are light and fluffy, then stir in the melted chocolate. Add the eggs, one at a time, beating well after each is added. Stir in the flour gradually. Fold in the pecans and vanilla and pour into 2 nonstick 8-inch square cake pans. Bake at 325° for 25 minutes. Cool in the pans for 5 minutes, and remove to wire racks.

To make the frosting, combine the sugar, milk, salt, chocolate, and shortening in a heavy saucepan. Cook the mixture over low heat until it begins to boil and the sugar dissolves, stirring constantly. Boil for another 3 minutes, but do not stir; remove the frosting from the heat. Let it stand to cool for several minutes, then add the vanilla, beating until it is firm enough to spread on the cake. You may add a few drops of cream to thin the frosting slightly if it becomes too firm.

Makes 8 to 10 servings.

Mocha Madness Chocolate Cake

1¾   cups all-purpose flour
1   cup granulated sugar
¾   cup unsweetened cocoa powder
1½   teaspoons baking soda
1½   teaspoons salt
1¼   cups buttermilk
1   cup packed brown sugar
2   eggs, lightly beaten
¼   cup canola oil
2   teaspoons vanilla extract
¾   cup hot, strong black coffee

Icing:
1   cup confectioners' sugar
½   teaspoon vanilla extract
1   to 2 tablespoons buttermilk

Preheat the oven to 350°. Spray a 12-cup bundt or tube pan with cooking spray. Dust the pan with flour and shake out the excess.

In a large bowl, whisk together the flour, sugar, cocoa, baking soda, baking powder, and salt. Add the buttermilk, brown sugar, eggs, oil, and vanilla and beat with an electric mixer on high for 2 minutes. Whisk in the hot coffee. Pour the batter into the pan and bake for 45 to 50 minutes until a tester comes out clean. Cool the cake in the pan, then invert it onto a wire rack to cool completely.

For the icing, whisk together the sugar, vanilla, and enough buttermilk to make icing just thin enough to drizzle over the cake and have it run down the sides.

Makes 12 servings.

Chocolate Pizza
It doesn't get much better than this!!

Crust:
1   box Nabisco Famous Chocolate Wafers, crushed
½   cup sugar
3   tablespoons all-purpose flour
½   cup melted butter

In a bowl, mix all the ingredients and press them into a buttered or greased 10-inch spring form pan. Bake at 325° for about 20 minutes.

Filling:
8   ounces cream cheese, softened
1   4.6-ounce package vanilla instant pudding
3   tablespoons sugar
¾   cup cold milk

In a mixing bowl, beat all ingredients until they are light and fluffy. Spread the filling over the chocolate crust.

Sauce:
¾   cup raspberries
2   tablespoons sugar

In a mixing bowl, purée the raspberries and strain. Mix in the sugar and spread the sauce over the filling.

Toppings
½   cup blueberries
1   banana, sliced
½   cup raspberries
2   kiwis, peeled and sliced
½   cup strawberries
½   cup apricot preserves, beaten
     Caramel sauce
     Shaved white chocolate

Spread the fresh fruit over the top of the pizza and brush with the beaten apricot preserves to glaze. Drizzle the top with the caramel sauce and top with the shaved white chocolate.

Makes 1 pizza.

Mississippi Mud Ice Cream

I use this recipe when my church has homemade ice cream socials. It always makes a big splash!

1	*tablespoon instant coffee granules*
1	*cup hot water*
2	*14-ounce cans chocolate sweetened condensed milk*
1	*quart whipping cream*
2	*cups chopped pecans, toasted*
1	*cup miniature marshmallows*

In a large mixing bowl, dissolve the coffee granules in the hot water, then cool slightly. Stir together the coffee, condensed milk, and whipping cream and pour into the freezer container of a 1-gallon electric ice cream freezer. Freeze according to the manufacturer's instructions.

Once the ice cream is made, open the freezing container and stir in the chopped pecans and marshmallows. Close the freezer again and pack it with additional ice and rock salt. Let the ice cream stand 1 hour before serving, if desired.

Make 3 quarts of ice cream.

Gilligan's Island Coconut Cream Pie

This comes out perfect every time, so I count on it often for my special guests.

⅓	cup all-purpose flour
1	cup sugar
1	teaspoon salt
3	eggs, separated
2	cups half and half
2	teaspoons vanilla extract
3	tablespoons butter
1	cup flaked coconut
1	9-inch baked pie shell
1	cup sugar
1	cup corn syrup

In a medium bowl, sift the flour, sugar, and salt together. In a small bowl, whip the egg yolks and gradually stir in the half and half, whisking with a wire whisk. When they are thoroughly mixed, add the liquid mixture to the flour mixture, stirring gently and constantly until well blended. Microwave at 1-minute intervals on high, stirring between each interval. Do this approximately three times or until thick.

Remove the mixture from the microwave, add the butter, and let it melt. When the mixture is cooled, add the vanilla and coconut. Pour it into the pie shell.

To make the meringue, beat the egg whites in a clean, cool bowl until they are fluffy. Gradually add the sugar and then the corn syrup. Whip them until they are stiff. Spoon the meringue on top of the pie and sprinkle the top with coconut. Brown in a 350° oven until the pie is golden brown. Cool and serve.

Makes 6 to 8 servings.

Jeanne's Famous Pumpkin Flan

2 *cups pumpkin pie filling*
1 *14-ounce can sweetened condensed milk*
4 *large eggs*
⅓ *cup water*
  Ground nutmeg (optional)

In a medium mixing bowl, beat the pie filling, condensed milk, eggs, and water with an electric mixer at medium speed until the mixture is smooth. Pour the batter into a lightly greased 8-inch round cake pan, cover with aluminum foil, and place in a larger shallow pan. Pour hot water into the large pan to a depth of 1 inch. Bake, covered, at 325° for 1 hour and 30 minutes or until a knife inserted in the center comes out clean.

Remove the pan from the water, uncover, and cool on a wire rack for at least 30 minutes. Cover and chill for 8 hours or overnight. Loosen the edges of the flan with a metal spatula and invert it onto a serving plate. Sprinkle with nutmeg, if desired.

Makes 1 8-inch flan.

With Roy Acuff

Festive, Fruity Parfaits

1   8-ounce package cream cheese, softened
1   14-ounce can sweetened condensed milk
1   12-ounce container cranberry-raspberry crushed fruit or 1
     cup raspberry preserves
1   9-ounce container reduced-fat frozen whipped topping,
     thawed and divided
1   10-inch angel food cake, cut into 1-inch cubes

In the bowl of an electric mixer, beat the cream cheese at medium speed until smooth; add the condensed milk and crushed fruit, beating until the ingredients are blended. Fold in 2 cups of the whipped topping and chill for 30 minutes.

Layer the fruit mixture alternately with the cake cubes into 8 dessert glasses, beginning and ending with the fruit mixture. Dollop each glass with the remaining whipped topping. Cover and chill.

Makes 8 servings.

With Garth Brooks and Dottie West

Chocolate Cheesecake Squares

I make these as a hostess gift when I am invited to dinner at a friend's home.

2	cups chocolate cookie crumbs
¼	cup sugar
½	cup butter or margarine, melted
2	8-ounce packages cream cheese, softened
1	14-ounce can chocolate sweetened condensed milk
3	large eggs
⅓	cup coffee liqueur (optional)

In a medium bowl, stir together the cookie crumbs, sugar, and melted butter or margarine and press firmly on the bottom of a 13x9-inch pan.

In a medium bowl, beat the cream cheese at medium speed with an electric mixer until it is fluffy. Gradually beat in the condensed milk until the mixture is smooth. Stir in the eggs and liqueur and pour the batter over the crust. Bake at 300° for 30 to 40 minutes, or until the center is set. Cool on a wire rack, chilling for at least 1 hour. Cut into 2-inch squares and refrigerate them until you are ready to serve them.

Makes 2 dozen squares.

With Dottie West

Raisin Bread Pudding with Bourbon Sauce

I borrowed this recipe from a friend in Kentucky. I just can't resist making it in Tennessee.

12	*raisin bread slices, torn into pieces*
1	*14-ounce can sweetened condensed milk*
¾	*cup hot water*
4	*large eggs*
2	*teaspoons vanilla extract*
¼	*teaspoon ground cinnamon*
¼	*teaspoon ground nutmeg*

Bourbon Sauce:

1	*14-ounce can sweetened condensed milk*
¼	*cup butter or margarine*
¼	*to ⅓ cup bourbon*
1	*teaspoon vanilla extract*

Place the raisin bread pieces in a lightly-greased 8-inch square baking dish. In a mixing bowl, stir together the condensed milk, water, eggs, vanilla, cinnamon, and nutmeg and pour over the bread pieces. Place the dish in a larger shallow pan and add hot water to the pan until it reaches a depth of 1 inch. Bake at 350° for 35 to 40 minutes or until a knife inserted in the center of the pudding comes out clean. Serve with the warm bourbon sauce.

In a medium saucepan, cook the condensed milk and butter over low heat until the butter melts. Remove the sauce from the heat and stir in the bourbon and vanilla. Serve warm. Makes 1½ cups of sauce.

Makes 8 servings

Flourless Chocolate-Almond Torte

½   cup butter or margarine, cut into pieces
1   8-ounce package semisweet chocolate squares, chopped
12   fudge-covered shortbread cookies, finely crushed
3   tablespoons slivered almonds
6   vanilla wafers
¾   cup sugar
4   large eggs
½   teaspoon almond extract
3   tablespoons confectioners' sugar, divided
1   cup whipping cream
     Garnishes: chocolate curls, fresh mint sprigs

Preheat the oven to 350°. In a 1-quart liquid measuring cup, combine the butter and chocolate and microwave on high for 1 minute or until melted, stirring once. Let it stand for 15 minutes.

Press the crushed shortbread cookies evenly into the bottom of a greased and floured 8-inch spring form pan. Process the almonds, vanilla wafers, and granulated sugar in a food processor until finely ground, stopping once to scrape down the sides. Transfer the mixture to a bowl. Add the eggs, one at a time, stirring just until they are blended after each addition. Stir in the chocolate mixture and almond extract and pour into the prepared crust. Bake for 40 minutes or until set. Cool completely.

Remove the sides from the pan and sprinkle the torte with 1 tablespoon of confectioners' sugar. Beat the whipping cream and remaining 2 tablespoons of confectioners' sugar in a mixing bowl with an electric mixer until soft peaks form and serve on top of the torte. Garnish with the chocolate curls or mint sprigs if desired.

Makes 8 to 10 torts.

Cranberry Tart

When I make this for Thanksgiving, I make two and freeze one to serve on Christmas Eve after candle light service.

½   *15-ounce package refrigerated pie crusts*

Cranberry Topping:
¾   cup sugar
¾   cup water
1½   tablespoons grated orange rind
1½   cups fresh or frozen cranberries
¼   cup raisins
⅓   cup chopped walnuts, toasted

Filling:
1   8-ounce package cream cheese, softened
2   3-ounce packages cream cheese, softened
¾   cup confectioners' sugar
¼   teaspoon almond extract

3   tablespoons orange liqueur or orange juice

Fit the pastry into a 9-inch tart pan according to the package directions and cut the pastry even with the edges of the pan. Line the pastry with aluminum foil and fill with pie weights or dried beans. Bake at 425° for 8 minutes, remove the foil and pie weights, and bake for 2 more minutes or until lightly browned. Cool.

Bring the sugar, water, and orange rind to a boil in a saucepan. Add the cranberries, reduce the heat, and simmer for 7 minutes. Stir in the raisins and cook 8 more minutes. Cool. Stir in the walnuts.

In a medium mixing bowl, beat the cream cheese, confectioners' sugar, and almond extract at medium speed with an electric mixer. Reserve about one-third of the cream cheese filling mixture. Spread the remaining filling mixture in the tart shell. Spread the cranberry topping over the filling. Stir the liqueur or orange juice into the reserved cream cheese filling mixture; dollop or pipe it over top of the tart in a lattice fashion. Chill.

Makes 1 inch tart.

Strawberry Fudge Pie

Strawberries mixed with chocolate are a long time favorite of mine. This recipe is one of the best combinations that I've found.

¼   cup butter or margarine, softened
¾   cup sugar
3   large eggs
2   cups semisweet chocolate morsels, melted
½   cup all-purpose flour
1   cup pecan or walnut pieces
1   unbaked 9-inch pastry shell
1   21-ounce can strawberry fruit filling
      Sweetened whipped cream

In a medium mixing bowl, beat the butter at medium speed with an electric mixer until it is creamy; gradually add the sugar, beating well, then add the eggs, one at a time, beating until blended after each egg is added. Stir in the melted chocolate, then stir in the flour and pecans or walnuts.

Pour the batter into the pastry shell and bake at 375° for 45 minutes. Cool completely on a wire rack and spread the fruit filling on the pie. Dollop with whipped cream, if desired.

Makes 1 9-inch pie.

Peanut Butter Bon-Bons

Sometimes a little self- indulgence and pampering are necessary. These Bon-Bons do the trick very nicely!

1   *18-ounce jar creamy or chunky peanut butter*
1   *cup butter or margarine, softened*
1½   *cups finely crushed graham cracker crumbs*
4   *to 4½ cups sugar*
1½   *cups finely chopped roasted peanuts*

In a medium bowl, beat the peanut butter and butter at medium speed with an electric mixer until the mixture is creamy. Add the graham cracker crumbs, beating until blended, and gradually add the confectioners' sugar, beating at low speed until it is blended. Shape the mixture into 1-inch balls and roll them in the chopped peanuts. Store in the refrigerator before serving.

Makes 7 dozen Bon-Bons.

With Buck Owens

Hope in Dying

While reading the Scriptures one morning, I was moved to compassion by the story of one man in particular. His name is never mentioned in the Bible, and we are given neither the town in which he lived nor the place where he might have worked. His age is not spoken of, nor is a physical description given. Actually, there is not one thing to identify him as a father or husband or even a friend of anyone. Even so, he is one of the most recognized men in the Bible.

What he stole is not identified, so whether it was something significant or of small value we will never know. What we do know is that he was a thief and one of the unfortunate people hung on a cross to die at the same time as the most profound Man who ever lived.

Although I have read this passage many times in my years as a Christian, I was moved that day to write a song that tells the story of the last moments in that man's life. When the thief asked Jesus to remember him, he was given the greatest hope of all—the promise of life eternal. In each of our lives, if we can look past the hurt and pain to what our Savior did for us and why He did it, we will discover the real meaning of hope. In dying to self, we are birthed to a promise—a promise of life forever with the Greatest Giver of the greatest gift, life eternal.

I'd Rather Have Jesus

A dream come true: 1008 Valle Vista. After years of working to own a big, luxurious home, I'd finally bought my reward. It was very large, very classy, and it was mine. There was an Olympic-size pool in the backyard and a baby grand piano in the living room. White carpets, a fireplace, a huge master bedroom, and three more bedrooms made my dream home all I had ever wanted. A new Lincoln Continental sat in the driveway. I was at the top. My life was full of wonderful things I had purchased for my family and myself.

I thought all the possessions I had earned would make my world complete. My children were happy. They loved the house, and the pool was like a dream come true. To look at us, we seemed the epitome of happiness and success, but once inside the front door, you could sense something was terribly wrong. My marriage was dying, and I was deeply wounded by the deception we were living.

My husband was not interested in my ministry beyond the benefits it brought to our bank account. He was fighting his own battles and could not support me because his self-esteem was in question from years of abuse and denial. We both struggled with that. I loved the house and was thankful God had allowed me to purchase it. I found out early however, that it did not soothe the ache in my heart or fill the need in my spirit to be the wife, mother, and minister I desired to be.

I had no arrows to fling at anyone else. Their only target was my self-absorption. My heart had long been closed to nearly everyone in my world except Damon and Justin. I was an expert at looking into other people's faces and seeing only my needs. I wanted to be a real picture of God's grace to the people I spent my weekends speaking and singing to, but I had no idea how hard my heart had become.

God's blessings were all around me, but my spirit was in disarray. The turmoil was draining the hope I tried to cling to so desperately. I didn't seem to know how to change; for ten years all my attempts had failed miserably. In the struggle to have things I'd never had as a child, I purchased a life of emptiness and heartache. I remember one Thursday night, lying alone in the big plush bed in my bedroom, I cried out: "God, if You have to take everything away from me to make me more like Jesus, I give You permission to do it."

I had prayed that kind of prayer only once before in my life, when I asked God to allow my child to live, and in return I would live my life in service to Him. May I say, "Be very careful how you pray!" He hears you! I got my request. After the dissolution of my marriage and the bankruptcy that followed, I was left with only a few possessions: my children, my dog, and a desire to change my location as well as my attitude. I knew deep in my heart it would be the hardest thing I would ever do, but my desperation to be healed was overwhelming. That is when I moved to Nashville, Tennessee.

I am humbled to say I would not trade the following years of cleansing and healing for any worldly possession. Up until a few months ago, I hadn't owned anything since that time. I am now blessed to have a wonderful used car, which I continue to make payments on, thanks to a Christian man who owns a car dealership.

I recently purchased a home after years of renting. I am honored to remain in loving relationship with the two incredible children God blessed my life with, and these young men are still teaching me how to thrive in the light of God's compassion and steadfast love.

I've tasted fame and fortune, drifted down sin's dark tunnels in search of fulfillment, and wasted great parts of my life trying to fill up my wounded soul with worldly possessions, only to come up empty-handed. It is in the washing of my soul, in the scraping away of my hardness of heart, and in the regeneration of my spirit by a loving Father that I now stand full and emotionally healed. I truly can say without reservation, "I'd rather have Jesus than anything this world has to offer."

Lessons

As a young person, I hated having to learn some of the lessons given in school. I watched my children go through some of the same things as they were growing up. I don't think any of us are too fond of lessons learned by making errors or lessons that profit nothing. My family had the opportunity to learn quite a lesson after moving into our new home. The boys were playing at the back of the property when they came upon something buried in the ground.

Not long before, we had heard about someone who found a can filled with money in their backyard. We were all very surprised to find something buried in ours. The boys went wild. They jumped, screamed, and ran to get the shovel. I silently hoped it was not a large container filled with drugs or something terrible. A pig farm was once located where we lived, so the thought of pigs' feet or snouts or other equally awful things also entered my mind.

Damon and Justin took turns digging for the "treasure," which was buried at least three feet down. It was hot outside and the ground was dry and hard, so they came in to get something to drink often and rested a bit. They dug and dug for hours. From time to time, one of them would come in with a report on how the buried treasure was looking. As the afternoon progressed, so did the amount of red dirt on their clothes and in their hair.

Soon, they could see it was something big and round. After a few more hours, they came in with this huge industrial coffee urn. It was old and ugly, and they were so disappointed. I tried to console them by saying maybe we could find an antique dealer who would buy it, but it was so ugly nobody wanted it at all. Then they had to fill the hole back up with the dirt they had worked so hard to dig. We all learned that day that fallow ground might hold only worthless treasure.

As my boys grew into men, I tried to teach them about the treasure of knowing the Giver of all wealth and happiness. I believe everything we have and are given comes from the treasure of knowing and believing in God's promises to us. His gift of love is the ultimate lesson of life; a Savior's love freely given, and all we have to do is choose to trust in Him.

Learning to Touch

At forty-two years of age, I was starting my life over again. The move from Texas was long and hard, and the first years in Tennessee were a strain, emotionally and financially. We were learning many things about life in Tennessee. The schools were different for the boys, and they were having some difficulties starting over with new friendships.

It was extremely hard for Damon. He had just graduated from high school in Texas and didn't even want to move to Tennessee. We enrolled him in Belmont University, and he liked it; but he wanted to go back to Texas to be with his best friend, Jody, whom I have adopted as my third son.

After a year, Damon decided to return to Texas and attend North Texas State University so he could be with people he knew. It was difficult for me to let him go so far away from me, especially knowing he would have to make the twelve-hour drive alone.

I've always told my boys to be the best they could be, and I'd never get in the way of pursuing their dreams; so I had to let Damon go. As always, I was a basket case from the moment he left until the moment he called and told me he was safe in Texas.

For many months I cried almost every day. I missed him with every beat of my heart. I guess every mother goes through the same thing when her first child leaves home. It was the same when Justin left home three years later to attend the University of Tennessee at Martin. All I could do was blubber.

It's taken me several years to adjust to them being on their own, but I have, and I'm so proud of my two young men and the choices they've made in their lives.

Being alone, I now found myself with the need to work on my emotional well-being and my desire to be healed from the years of pain in my life. For two years I went to my wonderful spirit-filled counselor, Dee White, and attended several seminars called From Curse to Blessing created by my friend Craig Hill. Craig's ministry, Family Foundations, is changing lives like mine all over the world today.

I have always hugged and held my children, and played with them and kissed little eyes open and shut every day when they were small, but I couldn't stay in the hug for long. I would pull away after only a few seconds. I didn't even realize I was doing it. I learned in counseling that somewhere in my past I came to believe if I loved anyone or held on to them too long, they would leave me. This was instilled in my heart as a child from the day I was dropped off at the orphans' home.

It took lots of time and effort to come to the place where I could trust in the love others showed me and not run away from those who just wanted to love me for me. It was Christmas of 1992, and Damon was coming home from Texas for the holidays. I was so excited. I had invited some people I had allowed into my life to come to a party for the holidays, and we were all there when he pulled in the driveway.

When Damon came up the steps to the house, I ran and hugged him and just held him for a long time. His first reaction was, "Mom, what are all these people doing here?" Regrettably, while my children were growing up, I couldn't let other people into my world or my home, and most of the time they had to have their friends over outside.

I was anxious to introduce Damon to my guests. He was in shock. After a wonderful evening of fun and food, I walked into the kitchen to hear my son saying to one of my new friends, "Wow. This is the first time I have ever put my arms around my mom that she didn't pull away from me." I was so humbled I had to go to the bathroom to cry my tears of joy.

Later I told him what I had heard, and we had the most precious time of healing. I repented for a lifetime of pulling away, not knowing what it had done to his heart. Today I revel in the open love I can show to my boys and the love they show to me in return. When we do get together, we still hold hands when driving in the car and linger in long moments of holding each other. I will never stop giving the loving touch I never had.

I believe there is life in touch. I surely know this is true in my life. Jesus touched my life, healed my heart, and gave me the freedom to touch those I love.

Me, Justin, and Damon in the pool

Living Water

My sons, Damon and Justin, are great swimmers. I wanted to teach them to swim at a very early age because I am a water lover. The first lesson was a sight to see. Damon was about six years old, and Justin was almost two and a half. We were in the process of having a pool put in the backyard, and we watched with much anticipation. Every day the boys asked, "How many more sleeps 'til we get to go in the pool?" It took several months from start to finish, so the questions were relentless.

The big day finally came. Damon and Justin got up with the sun. We all did! I was just as excited as they were. I tried to explain that they couldn't just jump in; I would have to get in first and help them into the shallow part of the pool. Well, that went as far as the back door. I did manage to get into the water first but ended up with two arms full of little boys. They took me down with enough force to throw us all backward, which made monumental waves. What a sight we must have been, gagging and gulping and trying to stand up straight

I still laugh just thinking about that day. The boys were easy to teach from that day forward because their first experience in the water was a fun one. I thanked the good Lord for that experience. Soon we were all water wonders and spent many happy days in that pool. I taught my sons to swim, dive, and do tricks, such as an underwater backflip, which we called the Dolphin. They really thought that one was cool. It was a summer I am sure none of us will ever forget.

That water was life and joy to all of us. It reminds me of the living water Jesus gave one day to a woman at a well. Her life was troubled and sad, and she came looking for water to drink, not knowing she would soak up the Water of Life and be changed. It's the Living Water, from Emanuel's veins, that washes away all life's painful stains. Are you thirsty?

Perfect Timing

His little legs ran as fast as they could go. (For a six-year-old, that can be terribly slow if there's something you just have to have.) We were in Wal-Mart one more time. We pretty much lived there when it was time to get anything.

It was a jet fighter that consumed his thoughts today. You know the one: the Star Wars jet fighter, the most popular toy on the market that year. And as it was for every mother in America, my child just had to have it now!

I knew what this trip would come to. I'd already made the trip alone, but it was the only thing he'd had in his vision for almost three weeks. His big brother reminded him the store was probably out because everyone in his class was trying to get one, too, and few had had success. He raced through the aisles with great anticipation, not even looking at the other toys and games. Those little eyes were set on only one thing. Needless to say, when we left that store, two sad little men walked with me, and tears flowed like a raging waterfall. My heart was touched, but there was just no way I could tell them I'd already been there and had purchased the last two in the store.

The joy on their faces at Christmas that year was heavenly. They both got exactly what they wanted. I later learned that the night before they had snuck in, very carefully opened presents, and switched the action figures so each boy had the one he wanted, before carefully rewrapping the gifts.

The Star Wars jet fighter, right on time

So much of my life has been a struggle of timing and trying to learn how important time is. God's timing is the hardest thing to adjust to, especially when you have decided on a deadline. When my heart is hurt over lost friendships or relationships that have surrendered to lies, I am left puzzled and frag-ile. I watch the enemy try to destroy my faith and leave my mind frayed when I lose sight of God's promises and timing in my life. It's so hard to trust when you can't see. There have been times when I thought, I just have to have this thing or I'll die, and later I learned that if God had allowed me what I wanted, I would have died.

I am still learning that He knows what is best and, yes, I still fuss with Him over my sometimes silly desires. Yet He continues to bless my life even when I disagree with His will for me. I am thankful for His love, which covers my doubt, fear, and hurried decisions. Sometimes we just need to slow down and let the sweet fragrance of unconditional love saturate our lives long enough to savor the goodness of God's perfect timing.

Prisons

In the early 1980s I traveled with a ministry group from Beverly Hills Baptist Church, located in Dallas, Texas. Our church sent many into worldwide ministries.

Larry Lea was a young man who could literally pray down heav-en. We all marveled at his ability to pray, and loved to ask him to pray for everything. Larry was our youth director at that time, and he went with us to visit prisons. It was always a time of incredible ministry and awareness of how blessed we were.

We ministered in prisons in Kansas, Texas, and several other states. We would all pile onto a bus and drive to these prisons. It was a time of great anticipation and prayer as we made our way across this nation. We sang and shared and prayed and cried all the way to our destination and again on the way home.

There were many wonderful times of healing and restoration when we went into the prisons. The first time I went, I was scared. I think we all were. It was intimidating and horrifying to see the con-ditions prisoners live in.

When the heavy metal doors opened and closed, we all shud-dered. The choir would sing, and several of us did solos. I would sing and give a testimony, then Larry would minister.

After our ministry, we extended an invitation for salvation through Christ. It was very hard at first, as all of us were rather shaken up by the rough appearance of the prisoners.

On one occasion in a men's prison in Kansas, we were sure our visit was absolutely unwanted and would have no effect on anyone. The men sat with no expression on their faces. Some looked at us, some stared at the floor, and others just appeared to tune us out.

We continued our service as normal, with some of us praying while others ministered. When Larry gave the invitation, every man in that room came to the altar. We were astounded. God performed many miracles that day in those men's lives. It was awesome, and it reminded us that God can change the hardest hearts, even when we are certain no one is listening to us.

I will never forget our ministry in a women's prison in Texas. This was where I would be sent if convicted of the drug charges I still faced. I could get a sentence of up to twenty years for my offense. I was terrified!

Everyone in the group was supportive and assured me they would help me if I needed to run out of there or fainted, which I just knew I would do. When it came time for me to sing and give my testimony, the presence of the Lord was sweet and comfortable. I had no trouble telling the women what God had done in my life. I told them there was a distinct possibility I would be sentenced to that very prison.

When the invitation was given, many gave their hearts to Jesus. It was a joyous time in the Lord. After the service, many of the women came up to me and said, "Don't worry, LuLu. If you come here, we'll take care of you and make sure no one ever hurts you."

The love those women showed me in the midst of their confinement and heartache was awesome. It's hard to pay the price for wrong choices we make because our wounded hearts often don't recognize truth. God gave me the miracle of freedom from my sins in that I did not have to go to prison. I was given ten years' probation and later went to Austin, Texas, to apply for a full and complete pardon, which was granted to me in 1981.

My heart goes out to those who are still paying for wrong choices, but I know in the midst of isolation and darkness, God can still change the hardest heart if we will only ask Him. It is in the dark valley of our circumstances that we grow, down where the dirt and seeds of life take root and the shoots of love break through to become the beautiful flowers of God's mercy and grace.

Reflections of Grace

In the past few years, God has strategically placed special people in my life. On one of my trips to Augusta, Georgia, I was invited to dinner with Pastor Cesar Brooks and his wife, Sherry, after my concert at the Maranatha Christian Center. Sherry is a remarkably gifted writer and artist, and she has created many specialty Christmas and birthday cards just for me. She is one of the few people I have been able to allow into my heart as a true friend. Cesar is a gifted and compassionate minister.

As we talked and began what would become a lifelong friendship, I was touched by this big man's heart. He is strikingly handsome. I have a great time teasing Sherry about that, because he is the most handsome man I have ever seen! During our conversation, he quietly asked, "Is there anything we can do to help you?" I replied, "You have blessed my ministry so much." He said, "Not your ministry, Lu. You!" It overwhelmed me. In all my years in gospel music, no one had ever asked me if they could do anything to help me. It was generally assumed that because of the past years of being a celebrity, I had no personal needs.

I was so touched that I couldn't do anything but cry. I learned later that Cesar was terribly rejected as a child by his father. His anger drove him to many of the same places I'd been and even farther. to a place where he not only endangered himself but anyone who was in the same space.

His testimony is the most salient I've ever heard. His merciful heart has added dimension to my life in so many ways. I am connected to Cesar and Sherry by ties of love and respect that require nothing but open hearts. They are what I believe Jesus called us all to be as friends. They have been there for me in times of joy, pain, and the growing of my heart.

We are bonded by the love of Jesus. It is that love, that truth with grace, that heals broken, wounded souls. I am still learning today that I can remove the masks of fear and trust in the unconditional love of Jesus. I am obliged to precious ministers like Cesar and Sherry Brooks for opening their hearts to unfinished hearts like mine.

I see Jesus in the reflection of grace they live daily, and it reminds me to look past the surface into the depth of the ripples of pain many are struggling to swim out of. We need to reach past our own comfort zone to the unsightly places of people who live in the shadows and are bound by the fear of rejection. We simply need to be reflections of love and grace.

Seasons

Growing up in Texas, I was never acquainted with seasons. I knew of only one: hot. It was hot in the summer, hot in the spring, hot in the fall, and hot in the winter. Yes, we did have days when the temperature was cold, but it never lasted long. We even had snow on rare occasions, then, quick as a flash, back to hot!

I remember waking up many years on Christmas Day to temperatures in the eighties. The Dallas area was always extremely hot, with little color. Things were either green or brown. I had no idea there were so many magnificent colors in nature until I started to travel as a young entertainer.

I'll never forget the impact autumn in New England had on me the first time I saw it. It took my breath away. I just had to sit down and breathe in all that beauty. It was many years before I moved to an area that actually had four distinct seasons. When I did, the first fall was amazing. The trees on my land were washed in the most brilliant colors: reds, yellows, dark burgundys, and bright oranges. Outstanding!

I now live in the Nashville, Tennessee, area. It is one of my greatest joys in life to experience seasons in Tennessee. I live in a large house that sits on a lake with my very own boat dock. I sit on my porch and listen to the water and praise God for this wonderful blessing to my life

The first three years I lived in Tennessee, it snowed on Christmas Day. I was like a puppy with his first toy. Just wild. I sang; I danced around like a silly-willy. I hugged my children and generally acted like I was bonkers! The seasons in Tennessee are just wonderful.

I'm sure there are other places where the seasons are just as vivid, but Tennessee has taken my heart. I love the seasons here. They birth beauty and life as the old gives way to the new.

The seasons of my life have been much the same. There have been dark seasons of hopelessness and strife. There have been cold seasons where I couldn't manage to see past my pain to live in usefulness. There have been bright seasons of forgiveness and acceptance, and seasons of a wounded soul's renewal, times of being mended by unconditional love and mercy that cover self-inflicted boundaries.

I am moved to celebrate the newness of my own seasons because of the love of so many who have been added to my spiritual family. God has given me precious friends. He has blessed my life with newness. My spirit soars in praise of seasons.

Precious Memories

After twenty-three years of filming *Hee Haw*, there are thousands of memories I hold dear. Some are so vivid they will never leave my mind. One day, a beautiful event was spread out before me. We were taping what was called "The All-Girl Jug Band," where the women sat on a wagon or stood next to it. I sat in a rocking chair, and my precious friend Minnie Pearl sat at the piano. We each had an instrument to play. Some had kazoos and some had stick basses. I and a few others held jugs, and we all sang and played or plucked or blew while Miss Minnie played the piano.

After the lunch break, we all streamed back into the studio. Minnie was the last one to come in that day, which was a bit unusual as she was always very prompt. When she came in, she was red-faced and it was obvious she'd been crying. Before she sat down, she began to weep again. I was horrified. I'd never seen Minnie Pearl cry, not once in all the years we had known each other.

It moved my heart to such compassion, I immediately jumped up from my chair and put my arm around her. "Miss Minnie, are you all right?" I asked. She nodded as if to say yes, but she continued to cry. I said, "Are you sure? Is there anything I can do for you?" When she finally managed to compose herself, she told me something very sweet.

In working with Roy Acuff for some fifty years and having thousands of photos with him and of him, he had never given her a picture with anything written on it because his vision was terribly bad. That day he had met her in the hall and given her a picture on which he had written something special to her, and it had moved her to tears. I was so thankful it wasn't something painful. Her tears were tears of joy.

Not long after that, I sang a song on the show called, "That's the Man I'm Looking For." When I finished, Roy Acuff, who had been sitting off to the side, came over and said, "LuLu, I believe that's the prettiest song I've ever heard. Do you think I could sing it?" I laughed and said, "Honey, I think you could sing any song you want to." He asked me if I had it on a tape, and I said yes. He then asked if I would give him one. The wheels were turning fast in my head! I said, "I sure can, sweetheart, if you'll give me something." He chuckled and said, "And what would you like?" I said, "I'd like to have a picture of you." He chuckled again and said, "Done."

In a few days, he came into the studio with a large manila envelope. In it was an 8 x 10 color photo of him, and he had signed it, "To LuLu with love and friendship, Roy Acuff."

It is still a cherished treasure. It may possibly be one of the only two he ever signed in his life. In return, I gave him my tape with the song on it.

From then on, he sang that song on the stage of the Grand Ole Opry every time he appeared, until the day he went running into the arms of Jesus. I had the privilege of singing that little song with Mr. Acuff on the show many years later.

I am thankful that I had the opportunity to know both Minnie Pearl and Roy Acuff and call them my good friends.

I love the way God puts people into our lives to make us better for having known them. It's even more precious to have the honor of knowing my Lord and Savior Jesus Christ. I can proudly tell you both of my special friends are with Him today.

The entire Hee Haw *gang*

Substitute Dad

I've never known the love of an earthly father. I've never touched mine, I've never seen him, and I don't even know what his name is. To this day, I haven't been given the luxury of knowing who my birth father is. I've often wondered how knowing him would have defined my life. When most people think of their fathers, they can relate to a smile or the touch of a strong hand, or even a kind voice speaking words of praise and love. I know that many don't relate to those things because their fathers were abusive. I can't imagine what terrible pain that brings, although I do know the all-consuming pain of being no one's child.

One special person in my life makes me think of what a father would be like. His name is Sam Lovullo. Sam was our producer on *Hee Haw* for almost all the years we were in production. He is a wonderful human being with a monstrously big heart. He was a mediator, a politician, a fixer of attitudes, a soother of loud misunderstandings, and we lovingly called him our godfather of the show.

When I was just a young girl with all of about two and a half years of show business under my belt, he became the father I so desperately needed. I had been arrested twice for possession of dangerous drugs and was quietly asked to drop out of the show for a while. The newly syndicated show's sponsors were concerned about the adverse reaction my problems might bring to our family show.

I was destitute, alone, and pregnant. For the next year or so, Sam took care of me, sending money every month to care for my needs. He would call with words of encouragement and assure me that I would be all right. That was the only time in my life when I even had a faint glimpse of what a real father must be like. Since that time, I have always held Sam in the highest esteem.

We are still friends today, after thirty years. I treasure his "not so present" presence in my life, as he lives in California and comes to Nashville only occasionally. I will forever remember and cherish him as the loving, concerned, substitute dad in my life.

Now I am learning daily how my heavenly Father has covered my steps through life. He has watched me and protected me, mostly from myself, and loved me into learning to trust in Him and His promises.

Although I am settled in my heavenly heritage, some days I still long to know my birth father. However, I am humbled that God lovingly continues to bring me wholeness through His Fatherly love.

Teddy Bears

I've always wondered why some folks just have to have teddy
bears. I know several people who collect them. I've never had a
teddy bear that I can remember, so I thought I'd just take a look at
the benefits of owning them: They are soft, warm, and snuggly.
They don't talk back, and they're always there when you want
them to be. They make you feel nice and happy. They won't hurt
your feelings, even when you feel it necessary to fling them across
the room. They don't care how you look or smell.

Sometimes they smell kind of funny themselves and look rather
silly. They never have to shave their legs, brush their teeth, or even
comb their hair, and still you love them. It makes no difference if
they have clothes or not. They don't have to be fed or cleaned,
unless, of course, they collect too much dust. And they never take
up your space unless you want them there. I've concluded they
would be a nice addition to anyone's life, as is grace.

Grace is never hurtful or rude, never cold or calculated. It is the
warmth that moves our hearts to forgiveness and mercy, the soft-
ness that causes us to do nice things when we aren't sure we
should. It's like having a teddy bear to share with someone when
no words are strong enough to cover pain. It's healing.

I think I have discovered something about teddy bears that I
never knew. It's time for me to have one! I think I'll call my teddy
bear Gracie!

The Gift

I had just come offstage after a performance of a one-woman show
I was doing in Branson, Missouri. There was a small gift shop in the
lobby where we would go to greet the wonderful people who came
to see the show. I loved doing the show. I loved the people and the
beautiful country I saw all around me. It was a good time in my life,
a time of blessing and precious acceptance.

As I entered the gift shop, I went around the counter to sit and
greet and sign autographs. When I got situated, I looked up to see
a very large man, who had to be at least seven feet tall. I kind of
fell back with a laugh. He was very big. He had dark curly hair and
brown eyes. He wore a red plaid shirt and looked like a lumberjack.
His hands were extended across the whole length of the counter-

top. No one could get in that space but him.

As I started to greet him, he took my hand in his and said, "You have been such a blessing to so many. I have come with a blessing for you." When he let go, there was something in my hand. I looked down and was truly shocked at what I saw. It was a gold medallion. It bore a beautifully sculpted image of Jesus, wearing a crown of thorns and tears flowing down His face. I was dumbfounded. When I looked up to say something feeble like, "I can't take this," he was gone.

I asked two little ladies standing there what happened to the big man who was standing in front of them, and they said, "What man?" I said, "The man who was seven feet tall. Don't tell me you didn't see him. He was as big as a house!" They looked at me as if I had lost my marbles. "There wasn't anyone here except us," they said, laughing. I jumped up right then, and we all began a search of the building. We checked the bathrooms and the parking lots, and the man was nowhere to be found. My children were there and said, "Mama, we didn't see anyone."

I still have the medallion. I believe that man was an angel. I don't know exactly why he brought me the gift, but I do know it is real. God's gift to us is real, too. So many think God doesn't exist or, if He does, that He surely doesn't care. The most precious thing anyone can give is the gift of love, the gift that makes each of us feel so complete and accepted.

What we often don't remember is that the greatest gift was the love of the Father, who gave His only Son as the blood sacrifice that covers even the darkest sin. In that precious blood, we are given life. All we have to do is accept the work already done. Simply accept The Gift.

Sisters

They say if you have one true friend in your life before you die, you are truly blessed. I am humbled to say God has allowed me more than one. My life has been blessed with several wonderfully true friends whom I have known for years. One of these treasured people is my friend Camille. She is more like a sister than a friend. We have known each other for over twenty-six years. I met her in Dallas at a friend's house and immediately bonded with this "kindred spirit." We have fought some of the same battles and traveled the same roads in our lives.

She, like me, is a "Big Beautiful Woman," with all the baggage that accompanies the title. She is the single greatest influence of wholeness in the midst of turmoil I have ever known.

As a young girl with problems, she was a true friend to me. When I was arrested the second time for possession of drugs, she was the one who took my child, Damon, into her home with her parents and cared for him. She has been godmother to both my children and friend and confidante to them as well.

My precious friend and sister, Camille

We have been connected at the heart for most of our lives. In times of anger, frustration, self-pity, and total confusion, Camille has been a rock of support in my life. She has loved me enough to tell the truth, even when it's something I don't want to hear. In my struggle, she taught me the meaning of self-respect. I have watched her move from an angry, confused, self-abusive, nonfunctioning person to one of the most together people I know.

Her influence in my life is still helping me learn to move beyond the past. She is a wonderful example of God's love for me. It was Camille who directed me to Craig Hill and his incredible seminars called *From Curse to Blessing.* They have brought so much healing to my life. It is Camille who constantly reminds me I can be whole and well even if I am not perfect to look at.

In watching her life, I am constantly reminded of how God's love is current and available to me when I am feeling so unattractive I can't look at myself in the mirror.

Camille

She is sunshine to my often self-imposed darkness. Watching her grow gives me the courage to look past myself to new lessons in wellness.

She is the one person who manages to make me laugh when I am bound by sadness, who can make me think when I am lost in confusion, and who can give me the boost to escape when I am stuck in my own prison. I am eternally grateful to a loving, merciful Savior who saw my need and filled it with a sister of His choosing, a sister I will treasure all my days. I love you, Camille!

The Ring

When working in the entertainment industry, sometimes you are susceptible to the idea that you must look wealthy. I hung on to that belief for a lot of years. I thought I had to have all the "stuff" that would make me look "grand." I spent a lot of money on jewelry and clutter to make myself appear the perfect showbiz type.

I had quite a large number of diamonds, some real, some not. It's easy to dress up anything with something flashy. I was working in Branson, at what was then the *Hee Haw* Theater. This was before Roy Clark opened his theater there.

The show lasted only a couple of years because of financial issues.

I had this incredible 8½-carat, heart-shaped diamond ring I wore onstage. It was exquisite. Everyone always "oooed" and "ahhhed" at the thing, and I just loved it. Well, one night while I was singing onstage, I looked down and all I saw was three prongs.

I'm sure the audience saw horror written all over my face. Somehow, I managed to get through the show without falling to pieces. But I will admit, after that show, the fall was a big one. I absolutely freaked, panicked. I wanted to throw up and eat everything in sight. To say the least, I was stressed.

Well, thus began the search of the century. My family, everyone in the theater, all the parking lot attendants, my secretary, and some of the other entertainers combed that place. They looked under every seat, down every isle, in the parking lot, in the trash, in the concession stand and the gift shop. We tore the motel room to pieces. We even took a flashlight to the parking lot in the daytime, trying to find that stone. For three days I had Branson in a panic trying to find my diamond. Its value was in the four digits, and I was in the fifth dimension. I was crazed!

Finally, after much ado, I realized I had to let it go. This, I must admit, was a very painful decision to make. I found myself on my knees beside the bed. I prayed and told God I released the diamond to Him, and if anyone had to find it, please let it be someone who could use it to feed their children or take care of their family. It was the first time I'd felt peace in three days, and I finally slept that night.

The next morning, very early, my sweet little secretary, Judy, knocked on the door. When I answered it she asked, "How much do you love me?" I laughed and told her I loved her very much. Then she broke into tears and said, "Because I just found your diamond!"

It was lying directly under the right rear tire of my car in the motel parking lot. There was not one scratch, not one speck, on that stone. We had driven in and out of that parking lot at least thirty times in those three days. I was so humbled. What a lesson I learned.

In life, there are times we have to give up our hopes and dreams, and sometimes our possessions, to learn of God's faithfulness. Our selfishness and pride can keep us from the exact things God wants to give us. I still have the ring, although I haven't worn it in years, but the lesson I learned will always stay strong in my heart. Things aren't what give us identity; He is. And if we will trust in Him in moments of uncertainty, He will always give us the best, even if we have to lose it to find it again.

"Though I Walk . . ."

As a young girl, I never dreamed of becoming a mother. I had decided not to have children because my life as an orphan had been so painful. I couldn't imagine what I could do to make a child become anything better than I was.

As I grew into an angry, confused young woman, my isolation changed my attitude about babies. I soon wanted to have a baby so I would feel the love of at least one person in a life of loneliness.

Therefore, being a child of the seventies, it was a perfect setup. I was a "hippie" child in a society of what was called "free love." There were no restrictions by then on the acceptance of "love children," and I wanted with all my heart to have a baby to love and be loved by. So I chose to have a baby.

I didn't believe a piece of paper gave me the authority to have a child, so I gave myself that choice. It was a wonderful experience to carry precious life, even as messed up as I was. I continued to do drugs the whole time I was pregnant. It never occurred to me that I was putting this little life in harm's way. I was too emotionally ill to think of anything except what I wanted. Even then God was watching, protecting the angry innocence of a wounded soul.

The pregnancy went exceptionally well for a body extremely invaded by drugs. When it was time to deliver my baby, things didn't go so well. My body wouldn't dilate after many hours, and the baby was having trouble breathing. None of us knew that my child and I would both be in grave danger. Time was running out, and there was no time to do a cesarean section, so they literally had to cut him out of my body.

In the rush to save his life, I was butchered, leaving my body even more unable to function correctly. Six months later I would have to have what was called a repair surgery, after which I was taken to a room in the hospital. As I opened my eyes, I looked toward what I thought was the window, because it was very bright.

As I focused, trying to see the window, I saw him. He was slowly rising. He wore a long, flowing robe. His hands were extended, his feet bare. He was beautiful! I couldn't see his face as he was moving. I blinked my eyes to see better, and he was gone. Then I must have fallen asleep again. When I woke up the next time, I thought it must have been a dream until I wiped my hand across my mouth. There was something there. It was dried blood.

Later, I asked the doctor why there was dried blood around my mouth. He explained that I'd had a breathing problem during surgery, and they had to run a tube down my throat very quickly to save my life. I now know that what I saw was not a dream. It was real. It was an angel, and he had been in that operating room with me.

God promised us He would never leave us. I believe He was in that room with me there in the shadow of death. He sent his angel to stand around the bed of a baby Christian who simply needed His promise: "Yeah, though I walk through the valley of the shadow of death, I will fear no evil, for thou art with me."

Traffic

Traffic is something we usually don't want to talk about. I can't find even one person who has anything nice to say about it, myself included! I remember one thing in my life I just couldn't get around for a long time. There is a place where the road narrows to two lanes, and all the traffic in the right lane scrambles to get over into the left lane. It's a furious challenge of drivers and tempers.

For several years I, like most people, usually lost my temper each time I found myself on that road driving home. I heard myself say things and do things I didn't want to say or do. Then I heard a friend's story of his traffic experience, and it changed me forever. His name is Craig Hill of Family Foundations in Littleton, Colorado. His seminars of healing, called From Curse to Blessing, have truly brought healing to my life.

He told a story about driving on the freeway. Someone behind him was repeatedly honking his horn. Craig's temper flared, and he started to react when the Holy Spirit brought a check to his spirit by telling him that the occupants in that car were a man and his wife, who was in the backseat. She was in labor. The baby was breech, in grave trouble, and truly needed someone to pray for her. Craig was overcome with compassion and totally forgot his anger and began to pray.

What an incredible reminder of how much we need to be tuned in to mercy when anger raises its raging voice. That picture stays in my mind every time I drive that piece of road. I am thankful for the construction that will turn it into four lanes someday soon, although it is currently making it even more difficult to get through.

Patience is the picture I am painting here. I am still learning that patience is a precious commodity in a fast-paced world that just needs to learn to listen to inner aspirations. I am still mastering my skills at regulating my inner thermostat. I am so grateful God is perfect in patience.

Steadfast Love

Her given name was Magnolia Sunshine, but I called her SiSi. She was a mix, half Shih Tzu and half Maltese. She was solid white with big brown eyes and a precious little face. I kept her hair cut to teddy-bear length, with a topknot on her head. She was truly a sight to see.

I actually bred her mother and father to get her. She was the runt of the litter, one of three little females. She was my closest friend for several years, since both my sons are no longer living at home. I loved this little creature with a passion.

Me and Justin with Sisi

She was remarkably smart. She would sit, talk, go bang (play dead), and perform ballet, which meant standing on her back legs and twirling around and around. She was always excited to see everyone! She was an incredible alarm system (she barked very loud) and loved to meet new people. She slept with me every night. She had her own blanket and pillow, and when I covered her up she would stay there all night.

She was a wonderful example of unconditional love, as most pets are. I loved her like a child. She had on many occasions been the only one to listen to the pain that moved outside my heart into empty rooms. I am so thankful to have had her in my life. In my opinion, pets are God's gift to hearts that need comfort and steadfast love. She was such a blessing, and somewhere in the deepest parts of my heart I just have to believe that when we all move from this plane to the higher one, she will be jumping and running somewhere around those lambs that will lie down with lions.

In April of 2001, my precious SiSi went to run the meadows of heaven and await the day when we will both lie at Jesus' feet. I miss her with all my earthly being and can just imagine her jumping at the hem of His garment, singing loudly as she meets so many new friends.

She lives in my heart, and in my soul she will always be a medal of honor to the spirit of our little friends, given by a wonderful heavenly Father to help us along life's highways.

Unconditional Love

There is a man in my life who has left an indelible imprint on my heart. That is my pastor, Howard Conatser. He is the man who led me to Jesus.

I was a troubled young woman with an angry spirit, and Howard Conatser was soothing balm to my wounded heart. I met him when my friend Diane took me to church after my second drug bust. The first time I went to his church, Beverly Hills Baptist Church in Dallas, Texas, he literally came and got me from the back of the church and introduced me to his whole congregation.

I was mortified. I was full of drugs and literally freaked out! He stood about six foot three, and he had silver hair and the kind of incredible blue eyes that look like clear water. He was a big man and commanded attention with his presence alone. He had gentle hands with the longest fingers I'd ever seen.

His wisdom of God's heart was greater than any I've ever known. He was an ordained minister who asked God to "give him all He had," and I believe God did. I can't say he was perfect—no one is—but I've never known such a godly man.

When I first started to attend his church, it had about five hundred members. Before Brother Howard went to be with Jesus, that church had grown to over ten thousand. It was on April 11, 1973, that he led me to Jesus. I had been to the church several times and couldn't get over all the joy and peace those people seemed to have. I didn't know how they got it, but I knew I wanted it. It was a Wednesday night when I told Diane I wanted to talk to the pastor. She jumped up and screamed out, "Brother Howard! She wants to talk!" He turned the service over to someone else, and we went to his office.

Reverend Howard Conatser

I was scared, but knew I wanted what those people had. The first thing I said was, "I'm not ever gonna stop smoking marijuana, 'cause there's nothing it doesn't make better." I wanted him to know up front just how I felt. Well, he just sat there in that big chair and said, "God didn't tell me to tell you not to smoke marijuana!" I thought, Wow, this man must be smoking the stuff. They all must be, because they're so happy!

He leaned over that desk, stuck his very long finger in my face, and said, "God will take care of that!" I said, "Well, I'm not married, and I have a baby," to which I got the same reply: "God will take care of that!" I said, "They kicked me off *Hee Haw* for drugs." Same reply: "God will take care of that!" I said, "They're gonna put me in jail for drugs," and he said the same thing. I got so mad, I jumped up and started to curse and scream. I thought, Doesn't this man know how to say anything but "God will take care of that"?

I was angry and wanted to run, but he got up from his chair, came around the desk, and sat down on the floor with me. He began to tell me of how Jesus gave His life so I wouldn't have to pump myself full of drugs. He told me how Jesus could take all my pain away and give me new life. I literally saw my life flash before my eyes. I was in great trouble, my life was a wreck, and I had nowhere else to go. I was twenty-six years old, and my life had already taken me through men, money, sex, drugs, and even show business. Everything I touched fell to pieces, and all I had to show for it was the horrible mess I had made of my life.

He held on to my hands (even when I tried to pull loose) and began to pray for me. It was the first time I'd ever heard anyone pray aloud for me. I fell to pieces. All I wanted was for the pain to stop. There on my knees I gave my heart to Jesus. It was beautiful. Diane jumped up, praising God, and we stood up praising, too.

At first I hesitated and started to catch myself, and he told me right then never to be ashamed to praise God. He taught me many things in the years to come. Brother Howard simply loved me with an unconditional love I had never known before.

It took many months for me to give up some of the habits I'd acquired, but when I gave my heart to Jesus, He delivered me from the drugs right then and there: no withdrawals!

I praise God today for a man who loved me so much he didn't look at the person I was, but at the person I could become. He went home to be with Jesus some five years later, and I still miss him today. His unconditional love introduced me to the Author of unconditional love, and I will always be grateful for his presence in my life.

Three Hearts

I've often spoken of my belief in the truth of God's Word and that He has a plan for each life. In that plan, He can make His will for our lives available to us if we will choose to honor Him with our talents and gifts. I have been blessed to have many gifts.

I have always been a great cook. I have made candy for many, many years for my children and friends, and they have for all those years told me I should be selling my great yummies. In the second half of my life, I decided that would be a great idea; so with the help of a friend, I started to make some of my candies and began taking them to my church women's groups and other gatherings. I even bagged some of them and sold them at small flea markets and fairs.

Through this process, I encountered a young man named Marc Giguere, whom I had met previously at Gaylord Entertainment. We both worked for the company, he at Z Music TV as the head of programming, and I, of course, at *Hee Haw*. He and his wife, Jeanne, immediately became my friends and later became my business partners. Jeanne was working at another candy company in Nashville and was helpful in guiding me to begin the process of putting my candy on the market.

Originally, I called my candy "White Trash" because it contained crunchy goodies in white chocolate. I made it in my kitchen and put it in cellophane bags with ribbons and stick-on tags. Then we moved the bags to Jeanne's kitchen where Marc, who is a whiz at graphic design, created labels. We then started to use cute little boxes with stickers, and finally we could afford the full-color printed boxes we use today! I'm happy to say our products are in over 250 stores around the country and are selling like hotcakes! God has been very good to us.

I wanted to name our company "Three Heart Snacks," not only because of our three hearts working together but also for the Father, Son, and Holy Spirit, without whom we would be nothing and have nothing to give or contribute. Together, we have worked and prayed through almost three years of hard work. God has blessed us every day! My dear friends Charlie and Genie Wilson have also come on board with us and have been a tremendous blessing to the company.

There have been some tough times, some hard decisions, and even some lost relationships in the process. We have laughed and cried and prayed and praised, and through it all we believe that these three hearts will make a difference in many lives—with our candy, with our contributions to the Lulu Roman Orphans Project, and with our mission to help create better lives.

LuLu Roman's Down Home Parlor Treats now has four products, with more on the way. We are helping orphaned children and single moms, too. We desire to be a blessing to many, so could you please run right out and get some candy, now?

(If you're wondering where to find our yummy treats, check out our fabulous Web site, www.ThreeHeartsSnacks.com, for a store location near you.)

Index